Editor-in-Chief and Founder:
  Lyndon H. LaRouche, Jr.
Editorial Board: *Lyndon H. LaRouche, Jr. , Helga
  Zepp-LaRouche, Robert Ingraham, Tony
  Papert, Gerald Rose, Dennis Small, Jeffrey
  Steinberg, William Wertz*
Co-Editors: *Robert Ingraham, Tony Papert*
Technology: *Marsha Freeman*
Books: *Katherine Notley*
Ebooks: *Richard Burden*
Graphics: *Alan Yue*
Photos: *Stuart Lewis*
Circulation Manager: *Stanley Ezrol*

INTELLIGENCE DIRECTORS
Counterintelligence: *Jeffrey Steinberg, Michele
  Steinberg*
Economics: *John Hoefle, Marcia Merry Baker,
  Paul Gallagher*
History: *Anton Chaitkin*
Ibero-America: *Dennis Small*
Russia and Eastern Europe: *Rachel Douglas*
United States: *Debra Freeman*

INTERNATIONAL BUREAUS
Bogotá: *Miriam Redondo*
Berlin: *Rainer Apel*
Copenhagen: *Tom Gillesberg*
Houston: *Harley Schlanger*
Lima: *Sara Madueño*
Melbourne: *Robert Barwick*
Mexico City: *Gerardo Castilleja Chávez*
New Delhi: *Ramtanu Maitra*
Paris: *Christine Bierre*
Stockholm: *Ulf Sandmark*
United Nations, N.Y.C.: *Leni Rubinstein*
Washington, D.C.: *William Jones*
Wiesbaden: *Göran Haglund*

ON THE WEB
e-mail: eirns@larouchepub.com
www.larouchepub.com
www.executiveintelligencereview.com
www.larouchepub.com/eiw
Webmaster: *John Sigerson*
Assistant Webmaster: *George Hollis*
Editor, Arabic-language edition: *Hussein Askary*

EIR (ISSN 0273-6314) *is published weekly
(50 issues), by EIR News Service, Inc.,
P.O. Box 17390, Washington, D.C. 20041-0390.
(703) 297-8434*

European Headquarters: E.I.R. GmbH, Postfach
Bahnstrasse 9a, D-65205, Wiesbaden, Germany
Tel: 49-611-73650
Homepage: http://www.eir.de
e-mail: info@eir.de
Director: Georg Neudecker

Montreal, Canada: 514-461-1557
eir@eircanada.ca

Denmark: EIR - Danmark, Sankt Knuds Vej 11,
basement left, DK-1903 Frederiksberg, Denmark.
Tel.: +45 35 43 60 40, Fax: +45 35 43 87 57. e-mail:
eirdk@hotmail.com.

Mexico City: EIR, Sor Juana Inés de la Cruz 242-2
Col. Agricultura C.P. 11360
Delegación M. Hidalgo, México D.F.
Tel. (5525) 5318-2301
eirmexico@gmail.com

Copyright: ©2017 EIR News Service. All rights
reserved. Reproduction in whole or in part without
permission strictly prohibited.

Canada Post Publication Sales Agreement
#40683579

Postmaster: Send all address changes to *EIR*, P.O.
Box 17390, Washington, D.C. 20041-0390.

Signed articles in *EIR* represent the views of the authors,
and not necessarily those of the Editorial Board.

Bring the New Silk Road To President Trump's U.S.A.

EIR Contents

www.larouchepub.com Volume 45, Number 6, February 9, 2018

Graphic depiction of the proposed Bering Strait tunnel.

Council for the Study of Productive Forces (SOPS), Russia

BRING THE NEW SILK ROAD TO PRESIDENT TRUMP'S U.S.A.

THE NEW SILK ROAD IS CHANGING THE WORLD

America Must Join

Helga Zepp-LaRouche's weekly webcast for Feb. 1 can be seen at newparadigm.schillerinstitute.com This version has been edited.

Harley Schlanger: Hello! I'm Harley Schlanger from the Schiller Institute. Welcome to this week's international webcast, featuring Schiller Institute founder Helga Zepp-LaRouche.

There have been some quite extraordinary developments in the past days. I think the most important one, to start with, is the State of the Union address on Jan. 30 by President Trump. Helga, what are your thoughts on what Trump had to say and the reactions to it?

Helga Zepp-LaRouche: He did not say what he should have said—that he was adopting the Four Laws of Lyndon LaRouche—Glass-Steagall and a new credit system in the tradition of Alexander Hamilton. But we are not giving up hope that that may still come. Remember, after all, after my husband had campaigned for what became the Strategic Defense Initiative (SDI), President Reagan did not mention the SDI in his 1983 State of the Union address. But immediately thereafter, on March 23, Reagan publicly announced the Strategic Defense Initiative. In the same way, we hope and fight for this necessary turn in policy today—that when President Trump has to confront the question of financing the infrastructure drive he just announced, he will come back to his election promise to restore Glass-Steagall.

Otherwise, the speech was not bad. I think it's quite significant that, according to a CBS poll, 75%

of the people who saw the speech strongly supported it. I think that domestically, he definitely touched on a sense of optimism, even though there are still many problems with the financial system which he did not address. But I think it's on a good trajectory.

I think the strongest indicator that he is doing something good, is the freakout by the Democrats. While President Trump appealed for bipartisan cooperation on the immigration issue and on infrastructure, the Democrats just sat there, demonstratively not applauding. They have made themselves the war party. That has now become crystal clear, because the day before the State of the Union was the deadline for the implementation of sanctions against Russia that the Congress had voted up half a year earlier—but nothing happened! The Trump Administration did not implement these sanctions against Russia. There was a a violent reaction by such media as the *New York Times* and think-tanks such as the Atlantic Council, which accused Trump of

White House/Shealah Craighead

President Donald Trump, State of the Union address, Jan. 30, 2018.

House Memo Details Use of Steele Dossier to Spy on Trump Campaign Adviser

FBI headquarters in Washington, D.C. (Reuters photo: Jim Bourg)

by ANDREW C. MCCARTHY *February 2, 2018 6:37 PM*
@ANDREWCMCCARTHY

The memo appears to confirm suspicions that a FISA court warrant targeted Carter Page based on information in the dossier

refusing to do what Congress had mandated. But the simple answer of the Trump Administration on these new sanctions against Russia, was that they were not necessary.

That's very good, even though Trump called Russia and China "rivals" of the United States, rather than partners or something more positive, in the foreign policy section of his address—to which the Chinese reacted quite strongly: They said it was alarming and provocative. But then the Chinese Foreign Ministry spokeswoman said that the United States and China should work together instead, for a happier future of all of mankind. So their response, on the one hand, expressed displeasure—but on the other hand, they keep reaching out for the kind of cooperation which has already been demonstrated between Chinese President Xi Jinping and Trump.

The Russians responded even less harshly. One of their commentaries said that President Trump's speech was much milder than those of all of his predecessors— obviously referring to Obama and Bush.

So I think this is not the end of the world. It's not what it should be, but in the context of what is happen-ing in the United States, one can not expect perfection. Given the neocon mobilization, and given the really ridiculous behavior of the Democrats, I think he did pretty well.

Schlanger: Responding to Trump's refusal to impose further sanctions on Russia, various articles appeared saying that this just proves that Trump is a puppet of Putin. But on the other hand, the whole idea of these kinds of sanctions is counterproductive, especially if Trump is trying to pursue a policy of coop-eration. And that brings us to the Robert Mueller coup operation under way—there have been a lot of developments on that, in-cluding the probable release in the next couple of days of the Nunes memo. What do you make of the situation around this coup?

Zepp-LaRouche: I think this is reaching very interesting dimensions. As a matter of fact, after delivering his State of the Union address, Trump was asked, as he left the Capitol, if he would release the Nunes memo, and he said "100%." White House Chief of Staff John Kelly, who was also interviewed, said the White House would release the memo "pretty quick," because the American people should make up their minds on their own, on what their judg-

Andrew McCabe

ment is. And that is very good.

The German media—which had previously refused to report at all on this controversy, or *if* they reported anything, would only report it from the standpoint of Russiagate, and how soon Trump will be driven from office—now are trying to cover their behinds. They're still only reporting from the standpoint of the FBI ver-sion—but they do have to report the memo.

What happened this week was dramatic: There was the decision of the House Select Committee on Intelli-gence to release the memo. Then there was the firing of FBI Deputy Director Andrew McCabe, which is very good. Then the ongoing operation by Senator Chuck Grassley and Senator Lindsey Graham who, on the one hand are insisting on a criminal investigation of Chris-topher Steele—but they have also sent letters to all the leading Democrats, Podesta, the DNC, and various other Democratic officials, asking them detailed questions: What did they know about the Steele dossier? What contacts did they have with a list of individuals who were involved? Many, many questions.

McCabe is also under investigation, because it seems that he delayed the whole Hillary Clinton emails investigation by three weeks, to try to push it past the November election.

There is a lot of fury: There are people warning that the outcome of this fight will determine the fate of the United States. For example, Paul Craig Roberts, who after all was in the Reagan Administration, wrote a very stern warning, saying the stakes are extreme; if the coup plotters get away with their actions, then the United States will turn into a full police state, where the intelligence services will create a dictatorship, and the government will no longer be accountable. So this is clearly one aspect.

But on the other hand, the hope is that this memo, which is due to come out latest tomorrow, can really be an earthquake. Because if what seems to be in this memo becomes public, I think it will change not only the situation in the United States, but it will also have an earthquake effect internationally.

Schlanger: We have emphasized from the beginning the importance of going after the British role, especially as related to the Christopher Steele dossier and its promotion by Fusion GPS. And now it appears that there are people in the House and the Senate who are moving on this.

But what more can be done? We're continuing to get out the Mueller dossier that we produced. But what more can be done to make sure that people don't get diverted or distracted, but really home in on the role of British intelligence as the key force behind the anti-Trump move?

What You Can Do

Zepp-LaRouche: We are asking you to help circulate our dossier on Muellergate, because it is a question of justice. There is also a personal question involved: This same Robert Mueller was the head of the "Get La-Rouche Task Force" in the '80s. He is part of the apparatus which was responsible for sending my husband to jail for five years—even though he was completely innocent—and many of our American associates for even longer periods. And this was one of the biggest injustices.

Did Mueller Help Cover Up Connections Between Saudis And 9/11?

ANDERS HAGSTROM
Justice Reporter

4:55 PM 01/23/2018

Special counsel Robert Mueller may have helped cover up connections between a Saudi family and the 9/11 terror attacks, according to Tuesday report from conservative watchdog group Judicial Watch.

Court documents obtained by Judicial Watch show that as FBI director, Mueller

And it has to be remedied, because I repeatedly said at that time, and I repeat it now: The biggest crime was not only that my husband was sent to jail when he was when innocent, but the American people were deprived of his ideas and his solutions. I think that all Americans suffered because of that. If my husband had not been prosecuted and imprisoned by such people as Robert Mueller—and had been free to promote his policies—the United States probably would not be in the condition it is today. You wouldn't have this sort of drug epidemic, and you wouldn't have these kinds of economic problems. The crime was really committed against the American people.

And then there is Mueller's involvement in the cover-up of 9/11. That also urgently has to be addressed and corrected.

But the present operations against President Trump have worldwide implications! This is potentially a question of whether there will be World War III or not. So I think people should just help to get this dossier out widely, and make sure that it remains on the front burner until justice has finally been done.

Schlanger: To go back to the Russian sanctions for a moment, we just saw the completion of a new round of talks in Sochi on the Syrian Dialogue, where the Russians have been taking the leadership, and there are other countries involved. Now clearly, the attempt to push through new sanctions would undermine any U.S.-Russian cooperation. President Putin and Foreign

Minister Lavrov have repeatedly emphasized that they see many of the U.S.-Russia problems stemming from the Obama Administration.

If we could get past this Mueller operation, what would be the potential for U.S.-Russian cooperation?

Zepp-LaRouche: President Trump has repeatedly said that it's better for the world if the relationship between the United States and Russia is a positive one. I think that that is absolutely true, because then we could deepen the sporadic cooperation which we have seen in the case of Syria, and which we have also seen in the background of the North Korea situation—and then, hopefully, we could also start to address the Ukraine problem, which right now is still a very dangerous one. A zillion reasons speak for such cooperation. Anyone who has any sense of world peace, should be able to understand that Trump, in that sense, is a gift from heaven, if you compare him with Hillary Clinton, or with Obama, or with Bush earlier.

So we have to get this problem out of the way, where Trump feels boxed in. He's not totally boxed in, but he's forced to adjust to the pressure. He didn't veto the Russia sanctions you mentioned, for instance, because he knew that his veto would be overridden. Russian Foreign Minister Lavrov has made it very clear that the Russians understand the constraints against President Trump in the United States.

But once these things were to be removed, we could start addressing real problems like nuclear disarmament; like serious efforts to rebuild Southwest Asia; and solving the Ukraine and North Korean problems in a timely fashion. All of these things are impacted by the relationship between the United States and Russia in particular.

Schlanger: And Helga, what report did you get on the Sochi conference? It seems as though things did move forward on this. Is your sense that this is a positive development?

Zepp-LaRouche: Despite the fact that there was a sabotage attempt by some Saudi-sponsored groups that did not attend, nevertheless it was a huge conference,

Xinhua/Ammar Safarjalani

Staffan de Mistura (at podium), UN Special Envoy for Syria, in Sochi, Jan. 30, 2018.

with more than 1,500 delegates, and they established a commission to work on a new Constitution for Syria. I think it's very good, because they will now move on the idea—which is also in the UN resolution—that it is the will of the Syrian people alone which will determine what kind of government they will have. Now, this conference was fully backed by Staffan de Mistura, United Nations special envoy, and so I think it's both a big success for the Astana Process, and it is not in contradiction of the Geneva Process, but is instead an amplification of Geneva. So, I think overall, the result is excellent.

Schlanger: I'd like to move on to the economy, because that was one of the things that, even though the President talked about it a lot, he did not fully follow through with the policy that we put forward—and by the way, people can read our policy in a new pamphlet on the LaRouche PAC campaign for 2018, what's needed for the United States. We're seeing new signs of a financial explosion. Last week, the Carillion company in the United Kingdom collapsed, with 20-30,000 jobs at stake. Now there is a similar report on a British company called Capita, which may mean as many as 50,000 jobs lost.

The U.S. stock market is wobbling, the Federal Reserve is talking about interest rates going up. Where do things stand on the financial situation?

Zepp-LaRouche: One of the potential triggers is

exactly these corporate collapses, because these are large firms, and as many people have warned in the past, right now the corporate debt bubble is much, much bigger than in 2008, and it could be the trigger point. So this may already be the beginning.

Naturally, the behavior of the central banks in light of all of this, is just completely irresponsible, to say the least. In fact the European Central Bank is now considering issuing sovereign-backed bond securities, which is another way of saying junk bonds—as was immediately pointed out by the deputy faction leader of the Free Democratic Party in Germany, who said this is exactly what triggered the 2008 crash.

So I think all the schemes to keep the system going are not going to work. The Federal Reserve has announced that it plans to have at least three interest rate increases this year, which could very well be the trigger for the crash. At this point, we are straddling exactly midway between a hyperinflationary blowout, signs of which are mounting, one being the stock market bubble—and on the other hand the potential of a collapse if quantitative easing should stop. So if we stay in this system, we are in a Catch-22. The only solution is to go back to what Franklin D. Roosevelt did in 1933: implement Glass-Steagall, end the casino economy, and then go to a Hamiltonian banking system—call it what you want, you can call it the Reconstruction Finance Corporation, or you can call it the German Kreditanstalt für Wiederaufbau. Once you make the financial system sound again in this way, there would be absolutely nothing standing in the way of the full cooperation of Western countries with the Asian Infrastructure Investment Bank, the Silk Road Fund, and all the other financial institutions which are backing the Belt and Road Initiative. That is the only way to avoid complete disaster—that is what people should really help to implement.

Schlanger: As a sign of the bankruptcy of the economic reporting, Bloomberg interviewed, of all people, former Fed Chairman Alan Greenspan yesterday on whether or not there's a stock market bubble. Greenspan is famous for his statement that there was no "irrational exuberance," before several different bubbles popped during his tenure at the Federal Reserve. So, it's indicative of the problem that they still keep coming back to the people who caused the problem, to discuss the solution. Bloomberg should obviously be interviewing your husband, who is the one who not only forecast these bubbles popping, but who has a solution.

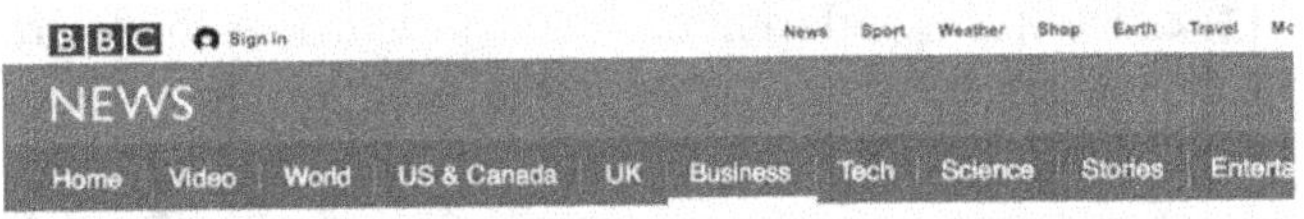

Carillion collapse: UK puts up £100m to back Carillion contractor loans

Contractors affected by the collapse of outsourcing giant Carillion will be

You just mentioned the Belt and Road; there are some other very significant continuing developments in the expansion of the overall process of the Belt and Road Initiative: What can you tell us that's been going on in the last days and weeks?

Big Changes Underway in the World

Zepp-LaRouche: I think that the number of new projects which are being announced on a daily basis is just breathtaking. China is building a new deep-sea port in Nigeria. They're involved in many projects in Latin America—as a matter of fact, I think the New Silk Road Spirit has caught on in Latin America now, in the same way as it earlier had in Africa, where even countries which were previously more in the "Washington Consensus" orbit, like Brazil, are now very interested in Chinese investments in their infrastructure projects. This is also the case in Argentina, where the Chinese are visiting with a large delegation.

So the opportunities for countries to get the kind of credit they were denied before, is a winning dynamic. There recently was a very interesting speech in Washington by a leading Indonesian economist and military person. That speaker said that the American model of democracy as it was pushed in the past, is just not convenient for developing countries, which have many more benefits when they go along with the New Silk Road, the Belt and Road Initiative.

And that viewpoint is now widespread. I think this

is the leading development. Even in Europe, there are more and more countries which are open to this viewpoint. For example, the Chinese are building a high-speed railroad between Oslo and Stockholm. This is very good, because once it becomes a pattern that the Chinese are building high-speed railroads in Europe, I think it will catch on. We just had this debacle in Germany, where the first high-speed rail connection between Berlin and Munich took *26 years* to build! It was only 550 km long: The high-speed rail system between Beijing and Shanghai, which is more than 1,300 km long, took only four years! One of my colleagues in Germany made the funny calculation, that given that the Chinese want to have 45,000 km of high-speed rail by 2030, if Germany should build that 45,000 km at the pace at which they built the Berlin-Munich connection, it would take them 2,340 years, and be finally completed in the year 4500.

This shows you what the difference really is, and very concretely how the New Paradigm of the New Silk Road works. It is something which is absolutely doable, but it requires a certain intention to get the result, and only then do you get it. But where that intention is not there, as in Germany, which is becoming the laughing stock of the world at this point. If you look at the new Berlin Airport, which will probably never be finished, it's a sad sign of what is going wrong in the Western countries.

Schlanger: Someone else who seems to have caught the New Silk Road Spirit is Japanese Prime Minister Shinzo Abe. He's been very much involved in interesting talks with Russia, China, and even with South Korea. Is Japan coming into the New Silk Road?

Zepp-LaRouche: Yes. I would definitely say so. The Japanese Foreign Minister was just in China meeting with Foreign Minister Wang Yi, and they had very extensive discussions on cooperating in third countries. Today the Chinese Foreign Ministry issued a statement saying that the new Chinese-Japanese cooperation has implications far beyond the two countries, opening the perspective of joint ventures in third countries. This is very good.

It's one sign that a major industrial country like Japan, which historically used to be completely in the Anglo-American orbit for quite some time, can actually recognize where their own interests lie. Japan is a country which has few natural resources, and is totally dependent on large markets—and now the only available large, expanding market is that created by the Belt and Road Initiative. I think this is *very* profound: Because if Japan can in that sense find its own interest in collaboration with China, so hopefully can the United States, and hopefully also Germany, which has been sort of a holdout, sticking to the old paradigm. But hopefully that can change just by looking at Japan as a model.

Schlanger: Last week, Helga, we extensively covered the mobilization by geopoliticians, neocons and others, to build up hysteria against China in the West, which is continuing. Now, you're one of the leading Western experts on China as it really is, as opposed to the nightmare visions of the neocons. What is it that Americans need to know about what's driving China?

Zepp-LaRouche: There is a very interesting new book, the diary of a girl named Ma Yan, *The Diary of Ma Yan: The Struggles and Hopes of a Chinese Schoolgirl*. She describes how she grew up in the very poor northwest region of China, which is prone to droughts and other disasters, and how, through very hard work, she became, not wealthy, but prosperous with a good living standard. This is a very good example, because there is so much propaganda about China and its supposed intentions and so forth, but what people don't want to look at, and should, are the values which govern Chinese society. It is very much the idea of the common good. There is a central government which keeps absolute control, which is absolutely correct—if you have a country of 1.4 billion people, you have to have stability. And the country is absolutely transformed: You see the fruits of the focus on the common good, as compared to the exaggerated, individualistic hedonism which characterizes the West.

The Chinese people are devoted to accomplishing things. For example, recently, Chinese workers upgraded and remodelled a railroad station in only nine hours. What took ten or more years in Germany's "Stuttgart 21" project, China did in nine hours. And that is because they deployed 1,500 people to do it—and then they got results. They build railways by building the railway outwards simultaneously from many points, and in that way finish quickly.

In the West, at least in Europe, the infrastructure is in terrible condition, and then, on top of that, there are big delays at construction sites. These construction sites last for years—maybe you see two workers there for five days a week—and that's just not the Chinese approach. The Chinese say, "we have to accomplish that, and we'll get it done. We'll do it with a large workforce," and then you see quick results.

I think it is really important that people change their view of China's intention. Look at the countries which are cooperating with China, and look at how their people are becoming happier and more optimistic. I strongly believe that the Chinese are being totally truthful when they say that their aim is not to compete for hegemony of the world, or have some new kind of global system. I think that the Chinese offer of an alliance of perfectly sovereign countries working together for the common good and for the joint destiny of mankind, is absolutely truthful. We need a political discourse in the United States which is not tainted by geopolitical interpretations and wild fantasies, whereby people do nothing but project their own intentions on China or Russia, or both for that matter.

I think we need a real discussion of what the future of mankind should be. Can we have a foreign policy which respects the UN Charter, which respects sovereignty, and which respects other social systems, without nations trying to export their own systems? If we can do that, we can have a peaceful world. I think that as long as Trump is in the White House, and as long as Muellergate is being defeated, the chances that we will get there are actually very good.

Schlanger: Helga, you said, "this is an unstoppable dynamic—except, perhaps, by thermonuclear war." The Chinese don't seem to be greatly taken aback by the hysteria coming from the neocons; it's part of what they expect, and they're still continuing to move ahead, aren't they?

Zepp-LaRouche: Yes. Their response is, let's join hands with the United States for a better future. So, they don't react, even to provocations—which they recognize—but they take the high ground, and offer their model. I think this is very good, and is a reflection of the Confucian philosophy, which underlies the Chinese paradigm.

Schlanger: OK, thank you very much, Helga. I think that brings us to an end today, and we'll be back next week.

Zepp-LaRouche: Yes, till next week.

The New Silk Road Becomes the World Land-Bridge

The BRICS countries have a strategy to prevent war and economic catastrophe. It's time for the rest of the world to join!

This 374-page report is a road-map to the New World Economic Order that Lyndon and Helga LaRouche have championed for over 20 years.

Includes:

Introduction by Helga Zepp-LaRouche, "The New Silk Road Leads to the Future of Mankind!"

The metrics of progress, with emphasis on the scientific principles required for survival of mankind: nuclear power and desalination; the fusion power economy; solving the water crisis.

The three keystone nations: China, the core nation of the New Silk Road; Russia's mission in North Central Eurasia and the Arctic; India prepares to take on its legacy of leadership.

Other regions: The potential contributions of Southwest, Central, and Southeast Asia, Australia, Europe, and Africa.

The report is available in PDF $35 and in hard copy $50 (softcover) $75 (hardcover) plus shipping and handling.

Order from http://store.larouchepub.com

Trump Negotiates with Russia To Solve Crises

EIR Intelligence Team

Feb. 5—This past week, President Donald Trump has demonstrated that he refuses to allow any continuation of the reckless policies of President Obama, whose confrontation against Russia took the world to the brink of thermonuclear war. In one week, Trump has: refused to impose the new sanctions on Russia which had been mandated by an out-of-control Congress; approved the release of the House Intelligence Committee "Nunes" memo, exposing

Sergei Naryshkin, Russian Director of Foreign Intelligence Service.

Alexander Bortnikov, Director of Russia's Federal Security Service.

the criminal actions of members of the FBI and the Department of Justice in retailing British intelligence lies about Trump's ties to Russia; and, most important, he invited the heads of the three primary Russian intelligence services to Washington, to meet with their counterparts in Trump's intelligence team, discussing the war on terror and other crucial areas of cooperation, as well as areas of potential conflict.

This last point came as a shock to many Americans. It was announced first by Russian Ambassador to the United States Anatoly Antonov on Jan. 30, who said that the director of Russia's Foreign Intelligence Service, Sergey Naryshkin, had been in Washington the previous week for meetings with unnamed U.S. intelligence chiefs. The same day, that meeting was confirmed by U.S. Ambassador to Russia Jon Huntsman, indicating that CIA Director Michael Pompeo was one of the people who met with Naryshkin. Huntsman, speaking to the *Echo Moskvy* radio station in Moscow, called the meetings "probably the most important meetings on counterterrorism that we've had in a very, very long time, at the senior levels."

Also on the same day, Jan. 30, CIA Director Pompeo gave an interview to BBC. He was asked about Russian interference in U.S. and European elections, and he gave the official response, "I haven't seen a significant decrease in their activity. I have every expectation that they will continue to try and do that, but I'm confident that America will be able to have a free and fair election [and] that we will push back in a way that is sufficiently robust, that the impact they have on our election won't be great." This was reported around the world as a warning of retaliation against supposed Russian meddling.

In that BBC interview, Pompeo also said: "We are going to go out there and do our damnedest to steal secrets on behalf of the American people!" So, we know that Pompeo wanted to make clear that the Trump Administration takes seriously its responsibility to counter any adverse Russian intelligence efforts.

The more significant news, however, is that Pompeo was in fact holding intense discussions with the leading Russian intelligence professionals, to cooperate in solving problems—real problems, that threaten the future of mankind, including terrorism, drugs, and conflicts that could spark global war, rather than the absurd claims of Russian meddling and collusion.

In fact, as confirmed by both the CIA and the State Department on Feb. 2, not only was Foreign Intelligence Director Naryshkin in Washington, but also Alexander Bortnikov, Director of the Federal Security Service (FSB, the successor of the KGB), and Igor Korobov, Chief of the Russian General Staff's Main Intelligence Directorate (GRU). They held meetings with Pompeo as well as Dan Coats, Trump's Director of National Intelligence (DNI), and other U.S. intelligence officials. A Moscow-based senior U.S. intelligence official was also called back to Washington to participate in the meetings, according to the *Washington Post*.

The Russiagate mob went wild, frantic that their coup attempt against the U.S. government is falling to pieces. Senate Minority Leader Chuck Schumer (D-NY), in a Jan. 29 press conference, ranted: "We sanctioned the head of their foreign intelligence, and then the Trump administration invites him to waltz through our front door. This is an extreme dereliction of duty by President Trump." He said the meetings were likely to have had something to do with President Trump's decision not to impose the new sanctions mandated by the Congress on Russia.

Pompeo, in a letter responding to Schumer, calmly, but sharply, put the hysterical Schumer in his place, referencing the latter's suggestion that "there was something untoward in officials from Russian intelligence services meeting their U.S. counterparts." On the contrary, Pompeo wrote, "we periodically meet with our Russian counterparts for the same reason our predecessors did—to keep Americans safe. While Russia remains an adversary, we would put American lives at greater risk if we ignored opportunities to work with the Russian services in the fight against terrorism." He went on to state he was very proud of that counterterror cooperation, "including CIA's role with its Russian counterparts in the recent disruption of a terrorist plot targeting St. Petersburg, Russia—a plot that could have killed Americans...."

Pompeo also made clear that the discussions included efforts to resolve other areas of tension between the two superpowers, not just cooperation on counterterrorism. "You and the American people," he wrote, "should rest assured that we cover very difficult subjects in which American and Russian interests do not align. Neither side is bashful about raising concerns relating to our intelligence relationships and the interests of our respective nations." Security cooperation between the U.S. and Russian intelligence agencies, Pompeo concluded, "has occurred under multiple administrations. I am confident that you would support

CIA continuing these engagements that are aimed at protecting the American people."

State Department spokeswoman Heather Nauert made the same point in her Feb. 2 press briefing: "I can tell you in a general matter, if something is considered to be in the national security interest of the United States, just like other countries, we have the ability to waive [the sanctions], so that people can come in to the United States. It is no secret that despite our many, many differences ... with the Russian government, we also have areas where we have to work together, and one of those is combatting terrorism and ISIS."

Russia's *Sputnik*, in reporting on the intelligence cooperation, made the point that the visit could be seen in the context of statements made by Russian Ambassador to the United States Anatoly Antonov last month, when he said Russia is interested in increasing U.S.-Russian cooperation in the context of Russian President Vladimir Putin's initiative to establish an international counter-terrorism coalition. Antonov added that "the U.S. and Russia have no obstacles for such cooperation against terrorism, and drafting the necessary regulatory framework for agreements would ensure national security of both states."

It should also be noted that one of the most dangerous points of conflict between Washington and Moscow, that of Ukraine, has also taken a significant turn in the past weeks. President Putin's aide, Vladislav Surkov and U.S. Special Representative for Ukraine Kurt Volker met in Dubai on Jan. 26 to discuss a so-called "Dubai Package," in which the U.S. and Russia would work with the UN to deploy a UN mission in Ukraine's Donbas region, to facilitate a ceasefire and measures to implement the Minsk agreements, this time with U.S. support. Under Obama, the U.S. was not part of the Minsk process and undermined any positive efforts by supporting the blatant sabotage by the Kiev government and the neo-nazi militias on the front lines.

Surkov was quoted by TASS: "The talks' key topic was once again a discussion of the Russian initiative to deploy in Ukraine's southeast a UN mission. This time, the U.S. has brought more constructive suggestions. The U.S. Dubai Package, unlike the 'Belgrade' suggestions, seems quite doable, at least at first glance. We shall study it closely and will give a response in due course. After that, we shall invite Kurt [Volker] and his colleagues to a new meeting."

President Trump has also initiated frequent exchanges between the U.S. and Russian Chiefs of Staff, which were totally shut down by Obama.

The British Sabotaged the Second Attempt for an SDI with Russia

by Dean Andromidas

Feb. 2—In 1992 the British government of then Prime Minister John Major intervened to sabotage efforts by Russian President Boris Yeltsin and U.S. President George H.W. Bush to conclude agreements that would have led to cooperation on ballistic missile defense. Such an agreement to end the Mutually Assured Destruction (MAD) doctrine, would have led to the revival of President Ronald Reagan's original Strategic Defense Initiative (SDI), proposed in 1983. Lyndon H. LaRouche was one of the key architects of that project.

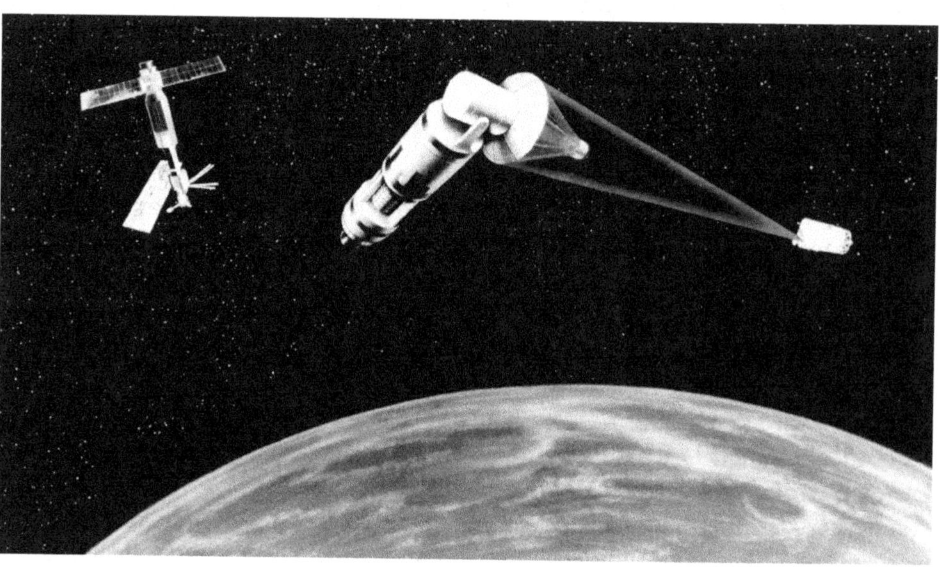

Artist's concept, space laser satellite defense system.

U.S. Air Force

Secret cabinet documents released last month by the British National Archives, reveal that Bush "was prepared to discuss sharing that technology with Boris Yeltsin, after they met at Camp David in February 1992, and declared a formal end to the Cold war." Material in the disclosed files includes descriptions of what the program would entail, including "a mixture of land-based and space-based systems," and "particle beam, lasers, and even chemical lasers to knock out incoming missiles."

The British documents expressed grave concern over Bush's communication with U.S. allies, in which he proposed that there be a NATO-led system, with Russia as the "principal partner." In response, Sir Stephen Wall, Private Secretary for Foreign Affairs in Prime Minister John Major's government, wrote to the Foreign Office, warning that America "assumed Russia would permanently be a good guy," adding, "We could not make that assumption."

A briefing note by British diplomats stated that their real concern was the end of the policy of MAD: "Any significant increase in Russian ability to detect and intercept our Trident missiles would make it more difficult and more costly to meet our deterrent criteria."

British diplomats noted that Washington—clearly under British pressure—had "taken to heart" the inherent problems of the East and West sharing defense systems, and backed off from the proposal.

British Feared Second SDI

Her Majesty's government had good reason to fear a new SDI agreement between the United States and Russia, because the Russians—by 1992—had fully accepted the proposals made by Lyndon LaRouche which they had rejected in 1983.

In a speech delivered in Washington on Feb. 17, 1982, LaRouche launched a campaign to ditch the so-called "Deterrent" nuclear strategy. MAD, which had brought the world to the brink of nuclear Armageddon, and to replace it with a strategy of mutually assured survival through the joint U.S.-Soviet development of anti-ballistic missile systems based on "new physical principles." LaRouche asserted that such a policy would serve as a science driver, bringing new technologies into the civilian economy and creating a foundation for unprecedented rates of economic growth and development. LaRouche's effort bore fruit on March 23, 1983, when President Ronald Reagan announced a Strategic Defense Initiative based on the principles laid out by LaRouche.

Parallel to this public campaign in 1982, LaRouche engaged in a back channel with Soviet officials to promote the policy on behalf of the Reagan Administration. While there had been significant agreement between LaRouche and his Soviet interlocutor on the feasibility of such systems, when Reagan announced the SDI, the Soviet leadership, under General Secretary Yuri Andropov, rejected it. The Soviet Union's leaders, LaRouche was informed, feared that the U.S. economy could readily absorb these new technologies, while the Soviet system would lag far behind, giving the United States the strategic advantage. Thus they refused to cooperate or to share these technologies with the United States, but would develop their own system.

In response, LaRouche warned the Soviets that if

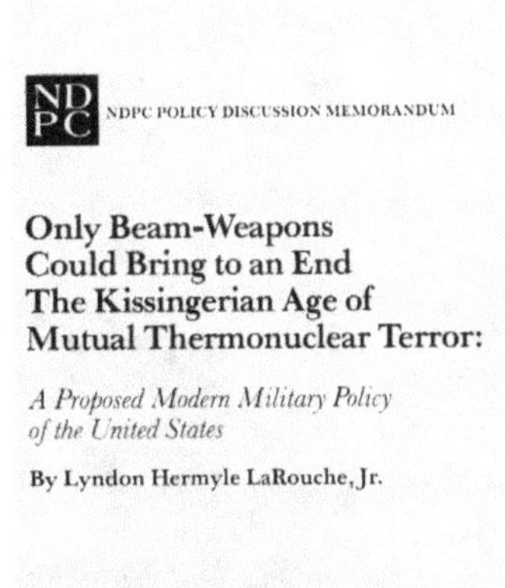

LaRouche publications advocating beam weapons defense.

they refused the SDI offer and tried to develop their own system and engage in a military buildup, the entire Soviet economy would collapse within five years.

When the Soviets launched a campaign against the SDI, they found ready allies in Britain and America who were committed to the MAD doctrine.

At a meeting with President Reagan in 1984, then Prime Minister Margaret Thatcher made clear that her government would support research but would not support any deployment or cooperation on ballistic missile defense with the Soviet Union. Thatcher clearly feared that such a policy would render Britain's own nuclear weapons obsolete. It should be noted that Sir Steven Wall, mentioned above, the Permanent Secretary to Prime Minister Major, who advised against a second SDI, had been stationed at the British Embassy in Washington in 1983.

As part of the effort to kill the SDI, a campaign was conducted personally targeting LaRouche. In the United States this was spearheaded by none other than Robert Mueller, the same Mueller who is today leading the coup effort against President Donald Trump. The frame-up tactics of Mueller, a member of the team of U.S. Attorneys, put LaRouche in prison in 1989.

The SDI all but died after the Reagan Administration. Nonetheless, by 1989, as LaRouche had forecast, the Soviet Union and its economy collapsed.

EIRNS/Dean Andromidas

Lyndon LaRouche, West Berlin, Oct. 22, 1988, forecasting the reunification of Germany.

The Russian Reversal

By October 1991, two years into the collapse of the Soviet economy, the Russian security establishment made a 180-degree turn on the SDI. The Russian government then was ready to propose its own initiative for U.S.-Russian cooperation, based on LaRouche's original design.

By October 1991 Yevgeny P. Velikhov, Deputy Chairman of the Russian Academy of Sciences and formerly a well-known Soviet critic of the SDI, and also of Russian ballistic missile defense, had changed his view. When asked if there was still Russian opposition to the SDI, he replied: "There are practically none among either designers or the military. The critics of such a proposal in both Russia and the United States are rather maniacs obsessed with old ideas and they have no influence." (See K.B. Payne, L. Vlahos and W. Stanley, "Yeltsin's Global Shield: Russia Recasts the SDI Debate," *Policy Review*, No. 62, Fall 1992, page 79.)

In January 1992, at a special United Nations Security Council meeting of heads of state and government, President Boris Yeltsin proposed a "global de-

Deputy Chairman of the Russian Academy of Sciences, Yevgeny P. Velikhov.

iter.org

fense system for the world community," to be "based on a reorientation of the United States Strategic Defense Initiative, to make use of high technologies developed in Russia's defense complex."

At that same session of the UNSC, President George H.W. Bush said he "noted the constructive comments of President Yeltsin here today, and tomorrow in my meeting with him we will continue the search for common ground on this vitally important issue. He responded with some very serious proposals just the other day."

Further discussion ensued at Camp David in February 1992, during Yeltsin's official visit and summit with Bush. Yevgeny P. Velikhov, a member of the Russian delegation, no doubt made a full presentation of the Russian proposals.

In June 1992 Velikhov penned an article in *Nezavisimaya Gazeta* outlining a potential proposal for a supra-national ABM system, which would be initiated jointly by Russia and the United States, and later be opened to other countries. The first step could be the establishment of a joint early warning system to be followed by cooperation in de-

President George H.W. Bush and Russian President Boris Yeltsin.

fense technologies and development.

Later, that same month, at yet another summit between Bush and Yeltsin in Washington, Yeltsin proposed the creation of a "Global Protection System" (GPS). It was agreed to form a high-level group led by Dennis Ross, then head of the State Department's Policy Planning Staff and Bush's chief adviser on Russia, and Russian Deputy Foreign Minister Georgi Mamedov.

This high-level group met in Moscow on July 13-14. As a result, an agreement was reached to create three working groups which would develop the GPS concept, areas of technological cooperation, and non-proliferation issues. These groups again met in Washington on September 21-22.

By November 1992 Bush had lost the election and the proposals died with the end of his Administration.

Why It Failed

We now know the British role in sabotaging that 1992 effort, which included orchestrating the collapse of Yugoslavia, which led to the subsequent Balkan wars, resulting in the poisoning of Russian-American relations.

The Russian proposal was doomed to failure by the "shock therapy" policy forced on Russia, the former Soviet republics, and the eastern European countries. The key target of this scorched earth policy was the scientific capabilities of the very military-industrial complex that Russia was offering to open up for cooperation with the West. The British-orchestrated strategic policy of NATO became the destruction of Russia.

If Bush had been seriously committed to the Russian GPS offer, he would have pardoned Lyndon LaRouche, releasing him from prison—and taking his advice, as President Reagan had done. Already in 1990, LaRouche had launched his Productive Triangle proposal to link the high tech machine tool capacity of Europe's industrial heartland—in the region bounded by Berlin, Paris and Vienna—to all of Eurasia by building a network of transport and development corridors, which would have created a Eurasian landbridge. Such a policy would have transformed Russia's high tech military industrial complex into a science driver for a blossoming Eurasian economy.

To prevent the significant interest in LaRouche's Productive Triangle policy throughout the 1990s from leading to its implementation, British Prime Minister Margaret Thatcher ensnared President Bush in a war against Iraq, which sabotaged the initial momentum. Thatcher then further undermined U.S. relations with Russia by pushing the notorious economic and financial shock therapy policy.

Two decades later, China launched LaRouche's policy, but instead of going from West to East, the

Development Corridors of the Proposed Productive Triangle

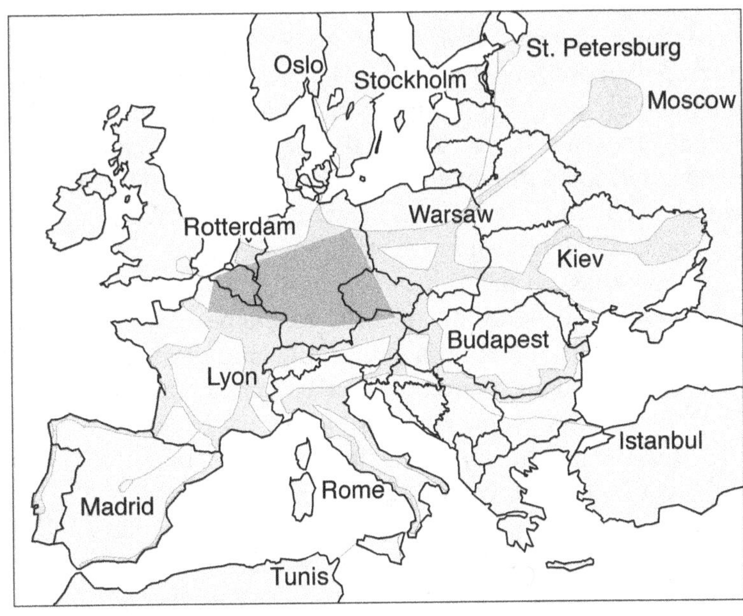

policy went from East to West, first as its New Silk Road and now as its Belt and Road Initiative.

A Third Offer for a New SDI

In April 1993, at his first summit in Vancouver with President Bill Clinton, Yeltsin once again made a proposal for cooperation for a new SDI. The proposal called for a joint development of a powerful, ground-based "Joint Plasma Weapon Experiment." This detailed proposal was made public in an article published in *Izvestia* on April 2, 1993, just days before the summit. The fact that this proposal was presented at Vancouver was confirmed by a senior Russian official, Dr. Leonid Fituni, of the Center for Global and Strategic Studies of the Russian Academy of Sciences. He revealed it on April 20, 1993 before an international conference in Rome on anti-missile defense for Europe.

Although the proposal did not appear in the final summit communiqué, its presentation was again confirmed in an article appearing in the June 19, 1993 issue of *Nezavisimaya Gazeta*, entitled "Bill Clinton Has Shut Down Star Wars: How This Could Threaten Conversion of the Military Industrial Complex of Russia." Author Andrei Vaganov stated that, according to Russian economists, the Clinton Administration decision to shut down the SDI program, and its failure to accept the Russian proposals, threatened to further undermine the Russian Military Industrial Complex (MIC). The economists, in almost the precise terms LaRouche has always asserted, said that economic breakthroughs, "paradoxical as it may be, lie in the internationalization of defense industry efforts and, to an even greater degree, defense-linked science, by posing for them a qualitatively new, single super-task. Many analysts in recent years have leaned toward the view that a variant of the well-known Strategic Defense Initiative (SDI), which acquired the unofficial name of the 'Star Wars' program, could be such a super-task."

Elaborating on the Yeltsin proposal, Vaganov said "The civilian economy and the MIC are Siamese twins: two individuals, united by a single circulatory system. The main economic interest of the MIC (under both socialism and capitalism) consists of guaranteed subsidies for the production of technologically complex products.... The creation of a global system of strategic defense ... would automatically presume the creation of a channel of guaranteed financing, without which the MICs cannot survive among nations." He said that an

White House/Eric Draper

Russia President Vladimir Putin (left) and President George W. Bush.

international supervisory agency was envisioned, which would have overseen "the gradual orientation of Star Wars from a military-political task to the tasks of the civilian economy, those of pure science, and the tasks of civil society."

Commenting at the time on the above article and Russian proposal, LaRouche said, "What you see in this article, is that Russian circles which are tied to the high-tech section of the military-industrial complex, and others, are offering exactly what I offered tentatively on behalf of the Reagan administration back during 1982 through February 1983, and what the President offered in his televised address on March 23, 1983. And they have come around to that. It is very interesting."

This 1993 attempt to revive the SDI has been all but written out of the history books, at least in the West, despite the fact that the LaRouche movement launched a major campaign in support of it.

Putin Takes Up LaRouche's SDI

In 2007 Russian President Vladimir Putin made a third effort to revive SDI during his summit meeting with President George W. Bush at Kennebunkport, where former President George H.W. Bush was also present. Putin proposed that the United States and Russia jointly create a regional European missile shield, instead of the unilateral deployment of ABM radar facilities by the United States to Poland and other countries, a decision which plagues U.S.-Russian relations to this day. While the proposal was taken seriously, it was never fully accepted by the George W. Bush Administration.

In 2011, during the Obama Administration, Dmitri Rogozin, then Moscow's ambassador to NATO and now Deputy Prime Minister, transformed the proposal for a new SDI into a call to create a joint program for the Strategic Defense of Earth, using the same technologies, "based on new physical principles," to defend the planet from threats from space, including meteors and asteroids.

It is now known that Her Majesty's government had been working all along to sabotage all of these golden opportunities to transform relations between America and Russia from the doctrine of Mutually Assured Destruction to Mutually Assured Survival and cooperation. The documents confirm that Her Majesty's government has been driving a wedge between Russia and the United States.

These same documents confirm that Russia had completely accepted LaRouche's design for SDI as a joint U.S.-Russian project to shift strategic doctrine from MAD to strategic cooperation on building systems of defense based on "new physical principles." They also show that there were policy makers prepared to discuss and even accept these proposals.

The threat of nuclear Armageddon that existed in 1983 continues to persist, with enough nuclear weapons to destroy the planet several times over, and nuclear disarmament talks are as futile now as they were then. The implementation of LaRouche's proposal for a U.S.-Russian SDI is as urgent now as it was three decades ago.

Unlike three decades ago, China's implementation of its Belt and Road Initiative has concretely put into place the economic development policy LaRouche has always advocated as the major complement to SDI. A new SDI will eliminate the danger of nuclear war while developing the science and technology required for the global development promised by the Belt and Road.

Call for Trump To Revive Reagan's Strategic Defense Initiative

by Dean Andromidas

Feb. 2—On May 5, 2017, U.S. Defense Secretary Jim Mattis initiated a Ballistic Missile Defense Review which is expected to be completed as early as next month. This is the first such review since 2010, and it has resulted in discussion in security circles about the revival of the Strategic Defense Initiative (SDI) that had been first adopted as policy by President Ronald Reagan on March 23, 1983.

Dr. Peter Pry, the former chief of staff of the Congressional Commission to Assess the Threat to the

wikipedia

Dr. Peter Pry.

United States from "Electromagnetic Pulse" Attack—has called on President Trump to relaunch the full SDI to replace the "dumbed down" version of ballistic missile defense now in place. Pry was also on the staff of the House Armed Services Committee.

In an op-ed in the widely read Washington-based daily, *The Hill,* on Jan. 17, titled "Trump must realize Reagan's vision for Star Wars defense—and soon," Dr. Pry described how Reagan's SDI ended the cold war, but had been sabotaged after he left office.

He wrote:

SDI technology was proven and ready to deploy. But President Clinton opposed "Star Wars" ideologically. Protecting America risked Mutually Assured Destruction (MAD) and 'strategic stability.' So Clinton's Secretary of Defense, Les Aspin, boasted he 'took the stars out of Star Wars,' canceling SDI.

What remains is the technologically truncated National Missile Defense that cannot defend allies and has Hawaii hiding in bomb-shelters.

We can win the New Cold War by resurrecting SDI and deploying space-based missile defenses. We are still technologically superior to all potential adversaries and can leverage that superiority to protect America from growing nuclear missile threats....

Space-based defenses offer revolutionary advantages over existing National Missile Defenses (NMD) that cannot protect U.S. allies or bases overseas, might be hard-pressed to defend the U.S. mainland against increasingly sophisticated North Korean threats, and cannot defend the U.S. from large-scale nuclear missile threats from Russia or China.

Most important, Pry stated: "'Star Wars' would render MAD obsolete, as Ronald Reagan intended, and really 'provide for the common defense' of the American people, instead of merely avenging them."

Pry points out that "Section 1685 of the FY 2018 National Defense Authorization Act (HR 2810) calls for 'Boost phase ballistic missile defense,' and Section 1688, [for a] 'Plan for development of space-based ballistic missile intercept layer.'" As in Reagan's SDI, both of those sections also call for "directed energy" weapons as well as interceptors.

Dr. Pry concluded: "If President Trump's ballistic missile defense review runs with these provisions, President Reagan's vision will be realized of replacing

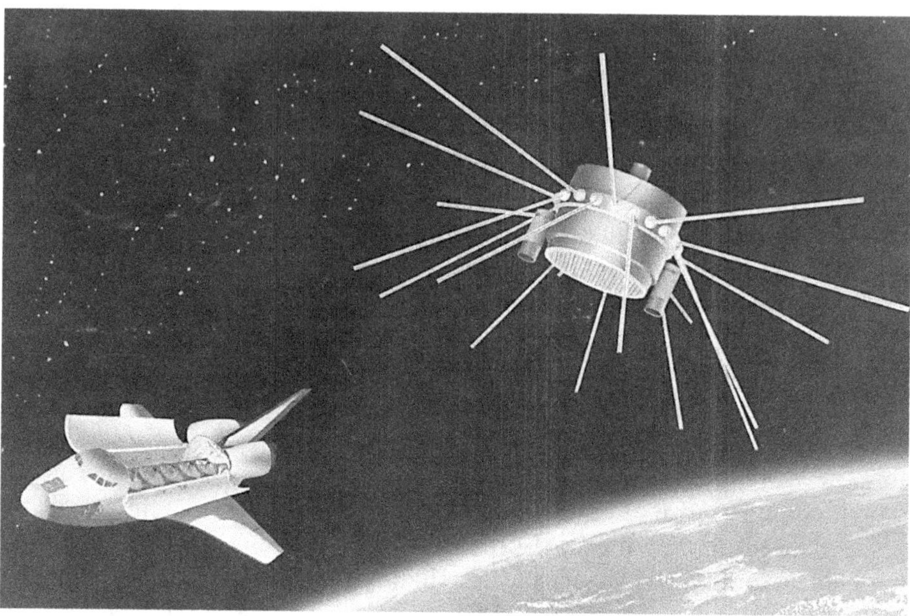

EIRNS/Chris Sloan

Artist's conception of gamma ray laser satellite, an element of LaRouche's proposal for space-based strategic defense.

the insanity of MAD with the humanity of 'Star Wars,' as will his legacy of 'peace through strength.'"

In a short interview with *EIR*, Dr. Pry confirmed that he is not only calling for the full SDI, including its "revolutionary" technologies, but also the need to cooperate with Russia to open the way for cooperation, as envisioned by Reagan.

Pry—as a Congressional aide—had previously worked with Congressmen, including former Representative Curt Weldon (R-Penna.), who were calling on President George H.W. Bush to accept Boris Yeltsin's proposal in 1992 to cooperate on a Global Protection System modeled on the SDI. Pry stated that Weldon, who founded the Duma-Congress Study Group, was one of the biggest supporters of accepting Yeltsin's proposal. In 2003 Weldon was targeted by the FBI based on claims of illegally receiving funds from Russia. While the ensuing investigation resulted in him not being re-elected, all charges were later proven to have been false.

Pry stated that although there is clearly support in the administration and Congress for the SDI, the current atmosphere created by the anti-Russian hysteria on the one hand, and establishment figures committed to so-called "strategic stability" on the other, could hold back President Trump from adopting a new SDI. Nonetheless, he emphasized, a fight is underway.

LaRouche: Beam Weapons Offer Americans a Military Means Toward Achieving Peace

Prior to President Reagan's March 23, 1983 announcement that he had adopted the anti-missile Strategic Defense Initiaitive as U.S. policy, Democratic Party leader and EIR founder Lyndon H. LaRouche. Jr. delivered on March 5 the following television address to San Diego citizens.

I want to talk to you about a very painful subject: the growing danger of a nuclear war between the United States and the Soviet Union. That danger is very real and, in fact, it's growing. I want to talk to you about what that problem is, and I want to talk to you about a possible solution to that problem. Some years ago, about 20 years ago, there were two events which terrified the people of the United States. First, there was the 1962 Cuban Missile Crisis, in which most people believed at the time, and rightly so, that we were minutes away from a thermonuclear exchange between the United States and the Soviet Union.

Then, approximately a year later, President John F. Kennedy was assassinated, and the fact of that assassination, the fact of the cover-up, terrified Americans and terrified people in Europe as well.

Under the impact of these two events, we in the United States shifted into a policy which was then associated with Defense Secretary Robert S. McNamara. (The "S" stands for Strange, and I think it's quite appropriate.)

This doctrine is called Mutually Assured Destruction, or appropriately, MAD. The doctrine essentially is that thermonuclear ballistic missiles are the ultimate weapon—a weapon so terrible that neither the United States nor the Soviet Union would actually ever launch a nuclear war. The argument is that we can eliminate war by maintaining static garrisons, static forces of this type, and by setting up arrangements which are in general called "crisis management." This means red telephones, special conferences, and so forth, to make sure nothing goes out of control, and that the two governments do not find themselves wandering by miscalculation into a situation in which they might actually set off a thermonuclear war. This MAD doctrine has dominated the West.

This led, by the time the Soviets began to overtake us, in the early '70s, to a process called detente, which was begun by the former mayor of West Berlin, Willy Brandt, and Willy's close adviser Egon Bahr. This resulted in the so-called SALT I and other agreements negotiated between President Nixon and Soviet Secretary Brezhnev. So detente was on. But no sooner was detente on than we began to move toward the actual possibility of a thermonuclear war. This surfaced in 1974 and has been increasing ever since. In 1974, we had what was called the Schlesinger doctrine, the doctrine that a "limited nuclear war" within such areas as the European theatre could occur without that leading to an actual nuclear war between the homelands of the Soviet Union and the United States. After the Schlesinger doctrine, we had other policies moving in the same direction, generally called forward nuclear defense. What these doctrines meant was that as the United States became weaker in its military defense, certain kinds of capabilities, particularly nuclear capabilities, should be pressed forward, closer and closer to an assault position with the Soviet adversary—in other words, that we should increase our bluffing as we became weaker.

Then, at the end of the Carter Administration, a policy directive was issued, Presidential Directive 59, which was the most insane policy in the series to date, and the policy which in effect is controlling the United States government today. This is an aggressive defense, involving Euromissiles and things of that sort.

In the meantime, partly because we are going into a

Ronald Reagan Presidential Library

President Ronald Reagan delivering his March 23, 1983 speech from the Oval Office, announcing the Strategic Defense Initiative.

depression, and partly because of the effects of the so-called environmentalist or Malthusian movement—the idea of trying to push us into a post-industrial society—our basic in-depth strategic capabilities are collapsing, both in the United States and in Western Europe.

At the same time, the Soviets are expending an extraordinary amount of their total product in developing not only the kinds of systems we are looking at in the charts I have here for comparison, but some absolutely new, fundamental revolutions in military technology, spending much more than even the CIA's Team B estimates of what they were spending. There is in fact a rapidly growing strategic imbalance between the two superpowers in which we of the United States are becoming progressively weaker and the Soviet Union is becoming progressively stronger. If this trend continues, possibly by 1988 or 1990, the Soviet Union will have a qualitative rather than merely quantitative net edge on us with respect to strategic balance. That is, they will reach the point that they can virtually dictate to the world the shaping of general international policy.

Now the danger is that sometime during the interval between now and 1988 or 1990, the President of the United States will be advised that this condition is developing; he may also be advised that it is too late for the United States to do anything to correct it. Under that condition the President has two choices; kiss the foot of whoever is boss in Moscow, or resort perhaps to using our thermonuclear arsenal for bluffing and trying to bluff the Soviets out of reaching this state of military development at which they would have a qualitative rather than just a quantitative strategic superiority.

This danger is increased by a policy advocated by the so-called nuclear freeze movement. Now some of you think the nuclear freeze movement is an anti-war movement. It is not an anti-war movement. The nuclear freeze movement specifies three things: 1) that the United States should cease all advanced technological development in military and other technologies; 2) that the United States should reduce its total military budget, but 3) that the United States must increase its conventional war-fighting capabilities for wars which shall occur below the Tropic of Cancer, that is, in Central America, South America, Africa, and parts of the Middle East.

We are committing ourselves to fighting Vietnam wars but not thermonuclear wars, at least so the doctrine goes. However, if we get into that geometry which the backers of the nuclear freeze advocate, such backers as Robert McNamara, Maxwell Taylor—who are rather familiar to us who remember the Vietnam war—we will be facing strategic inferiority relative to the Soviet Union, at the same time as we are massively engaged in Vietnam-style war or something approximating that, shooting our former friends in Ibero America, Africa, and elsewhere.

This madness creates a general probability for war, for thermonuclear war, during the second half of the 1980s. And if we continue on the present policy, then we shall lock ourselves into that geometry and we shall have war; it will be so probable that we dare not say it is not certain.

The Way Out

Now what I propose is a solution to the military side of this problem. My proposal is to eliminate the superiority of thermonuclear weapons as the final weapon. They are not an absolute weapon. We have had—over this same 20-year period—actual weapons systems and potential weapons systems with the capability of destroying thermonuclear ballistic systems in the stratosphere. We have had systems which could provide point defense to defend cities, to defend missile sites, or other targets from an incoming warhead.

The Soviet Union in the last six years or so has been

developing a set of weapon systems which could do this by means of laser-like beams, beam weapons. There are many kinds of beam weapons, and they are quite feasible now. If we developed a crash program now, we could probably in ten years or less guarantee that 99 and 44/100ths percent of a full flight of missiles directed against the United States would not strike the homeland of the United States. We have the imminent technological capabilities to do that. The Soviets have it, too. The Soviets are well ahead of us in developing such a capability, and some of the things you see them putting up peacefully in space are relevant to this. They have been on an accelerated program to develop this for some years, while we have been lagging.

Furthermore, not only can we eliminate that kind of missile, the land-based or air-based missile—that is, the missile fired from land or the missile fired from a plane—we can also potentially kill missile-carrying submarines. They say that submarines are undetectable, but that is a lot of bunk. We now know the technological means to pinpoint missile-carrying strategic nuclear subs. There are several kinds of technology involved; again, that is a technical matter, but it exists. So, if somebody tells you that sea-based or submarine missiles are invulnerable, either they don't know what they are talking about or they are lying. I know enough of the technology to know that subs are intrinsically detectable. So therefore it is possible to do this.

Winning By Default

If one side, we or the Soviet Union, were ever to emplace such a strategic system first, we would have won World War III by default. It now looks as though, with current trends from the Heritage Foundation and other lobbies in Washington, the Soviets, perhaps by the end of this decade, or perhaps earlier, will have such a strategic capability and we will have lost World War III. Perhaps we will go to World War III earlier, by the middle of the decade, in order to "head them off at the pass," as the boys say.

I have proposed that we change our negotiations on arms with Moscow in the following way: 1) that we agree to, independently but in parallel, develop and deploy anti-missile defensive beam weapon and supplementary systems; 2) that we agree to manage the progress in such deployment to such effect that we do not create a strategic imbalance of critical significance during the process of development; 3) that we then proceed on the basis of that agreement to a program of eliminating thermonuclear weapons, and 4) that we agree, as we put this into place, that if any third nation attempts to launch one or any number of thermonuclear weapons, we will jointly destroy those launched weapons—that we agree, in short, to free the world from more than 20 years of thermonuclear terror.

The Disarmament Hoax

There is no other way to go. It will be impossible in any negotiation to significantly reduce the number of warheads; neither the United States nor the Soviet Union would actually give up what it considers the capability to obliterate the other by nuclear means. Disarmament leads nowhere; it accomplishes nothing. We cannot eliminate thermonuclear missiles except by going to a weapons development system that makes them relatively obsolete.

Granted, there is the possibility of an arms race from such a development as I have proposed. That is true. We could go beyond developing defensive systems to developing offensive systems of great and terrible power. But let us hope that by avoiding and averting the immediate danger of nuclear war before us, in that process we might grow up a little bit, and then, having grown up a little bit, we might by then find ourselves acting like mature people to take actions to remove the causes of war rather than simply trying to stop the weapons.

I think the answer to this lies in what Dr. Teller said in Washington this past October—I agree fully with him on this. If we commit ourselves to this technological revolution—and developing beam weapons technology is a technological revolution in modes of production as well as military science—and we use this technology to assist the development of developing countries, to increase the general welfare of mankind on this planet, to make ourselves more rational, more scientific, more inclined to think rationally about the connection between policies and practices and the results of those policies and practices down the road, that if we commit ourselves to those things which are properly the common aims of mankind, perhaps in that great effort we can find a solution.

Therefore, I propose that we adopt this policy—a beam weapon development policy, and put together a crash program to do this. We must negotiate with the Soviets on this question, as I have indicated, and we must couple this with a plan for technologically progressive economic growth, to finally remove the hideous effects of centuries of British and other imperialism that blight the conditions of life for people of the developing sector. I think that is the way to peace, and I think that is the proper military policy.

March 30, 1983

Draft Memorandum of Agreement Between The United States and the U.S.S.R.

by Lyndon H. LaRouche, Jr.

On March 30, 1984, then-presidential candidate Lyndon LaRouche presented the following proposed legislation, which appeared in EIR's *April 17, 1984 issue.*

Article 1
General Conditions for Peace

The political foundation for durable peace must be: a) The unconditional sovereignty of each and all nation-states, and b) Cooperation among sovereign nation-states to the effect of promoting unlimited opportunities to participate in the benefits of technological progress, to the mutual benefit of each and all.

The most crucial feature of present implementation of such a policy of durable peace is a profound change in the monetary, economic, and political relations between the dominant powers and those relatively subordinated nations often classed as "developing nations." Unless the inequities lingering in the aftermath of modern colonialism are progressively remedied, there can be no durable peace on this planet.

Insofar as the United States and Soviet Union acknowledge the progress of the productive powers of labor throughout the planet to be in the vital strategic interests of each and both, the two powers are bound to that degree and in that way by a common interest. This is the kernel of the political and economic policies of practice indispensable to the fostering of durable peace between those two powers.

Article 2
Concrete Technological Policy

The term, technology, is to be understood in the terms of its original meaning, as supplied by Gottfried Leibniz, as the French translation of this same term, *polytechnique,* was understood by the Ecole Polytechnique under the leadership of Lazare Carnot and Gaspard Monge, and as the successive discoveries of Carl F. Gauss, Lejeune Dirichlet, and Bernhard Riemann provide an improved comprehension of the mathematical (geometrical) comprehension of Leibniz's original definition of "technology."

Technology, so defined, is understood to be the indispensable means not only for increasing the potential relative population-density of societies, but as also indispensable to maintaining even any present level of population potential. Potential relative population-density is measured in persons per square kilometer. The increase in potential relative population-density requires both an increase in usable energy supplies of a society, per capita, and also an increase of the energy flux density of primary energy supplies, and in the form of application of such energy to various modes of production.

The foundation of development of productive powers of labor in agriculture (broadly defined) and industry (also broadly defined), is the development and maintenance of such elements of basic economic infrastructure as fresh-water management, transportation systems, energy production and distribution, general improvement of the habitability of land-areas, and urban industrial infrastructure of both industries and populations' daily life.

Next, in sequence, is the development of production of raw materials by agriculture and mining-refining. All other physical-goods production depends upon the scale of output and productive powers of labor in these two categories of raw-materials production. Most essential, economically, socially, and politically, is the increase of agricultural yields per hectare and per capita, effected through technological progress in both infrastructure improvement and in modes of production employed.

Since developments during the fifteenth century in Europe, all advances in technology, all advances in the productive powers of labor have been based on the development of the machine, or on the design of processes analogous to the functions of the heat-powered machine in terms of other sub-species of physical principles, such as chemistry, biology, the development of electrical energy supplies, and the emerging role of productive processes based on principles of plasma physics. "Technology," as comprehended from the combined standpoints of Gauss, Dirichlet, and Riemann, treats each of these varieties of production-methods as subsumed by a common set of principles.

In all aspects of production excepting agriculture, and in respect to industrial goods required by agricultural production, advances in technology are transmitted into the productive process as a whole through the incorporation of improved technologies in capital goods, most emphatically capital goods of the machine-tool or analogous classifications. Therefore, the only means by which a national economy can sustain significant rates of technological progress, is by placing emphasis upon the capital-goods sector of production, and maintaining sufficiently high rates of turnover in that sector to foster high rates of technological innovation in the goods produced.

It follows that general increase of the productive powers of labor requires relatively high rates of investment of technologically progressive forms of such capital goods per capita in all spheres of production.

Therefore, the general advancement of the productive powers of labor in all sovereign states, most emphatically so-called developing nations, requires global emphasis on: a) increasing globally the percentiles of the labor force employed in scientific research and related functions of research and development: a goal of 5% of the world's labor force so employed is recommended as a near- to medium-term goal; b) increasing the absolute and relative scales of capital-goods production and also the rate of turnover in capital-goods production; and c) combining these two factors to accelerate technological progress in capital-goods outputs.

Therefore, high rates of export of such capital-goods output to meet the needs of developing nations are indispensable for the general development of so-called developing nations: Our common goal, and our common interest, is promoting both the general welfare and promoting preconditions of durable peace between our two powers.

The foreseeable direction of advances in technology over the span of the coming 50 years or longer is already clear in categorical terms of reference. There are clearly three general categories of scientific and technological progress on which humanity must rely into the period to come: a) very high energy-flux density, controlled thermonuclear plasmas, typified by the development of "commercial" fusion-energy production as the emerging, principal source of energy supplies for mankind, both on Earth and in exploration and colonization of nearby space; b) the application of energy supplies in the modes of coherent, directed-energy radiation, illustrated by the case of high-powered laser and so-called particle-beam modes; and c) new directions in biology, for which microbiotechnology is but a subordinated, but important aspect.

These three areas of technological breakthroughs define the role of powered, extended interplanetary and related forms of space travel, and of preconditions for life in synthetic, Earth-simulated environments of growing populations in colonies on the Moon, Mars, and elsewhere during the course of the coming 50 years.

Scientific cooperation in the development of these breakthroughs, and in respect to their applications to production and to exploration of nearby space, is an area in which the two powers must promote efficient cooperation between themselves, and with other sovereign states.

Article 3
Economic Policies

By supplying increased amounts of high-technology capital goods to developing nations, the exporting economies foster increased rates of turnover in their own most advanced capital-goods sectors of production. As a by-product of such increased rates of turnover in that sub-sector of the exporting nation's production, the rate of improvement of technology in such categories of goods is increased, with great benefits to the internal economy of the exporting nation. Thus, even were the exporting nation to take no profit on such exports, the promotion of higher rates of capital turnover in the capital-goods sector of that exporting nation would increase the productive powers of labor in the exporting nation's economy as a whole, thus supplying great benefit to the exporting nation's economy in that way.

The importer of such advanced capital goods increases the productive powers of labor in the economy of the importing nation. This enables the importing nation to produce its goods at a lower average social cost, and enables it to provide better-quality and cheaper goods as goods of payment to the nations exporting capital goods.

Not only are the causes of simple humanity and general peace served by such policies of practice; the arrangement is equally beneficial to exporting and importing nations. Only a profound ignorance of true interests of nations could desire any contrary policy of practice respecting "technology transfer."

Moreover, the general rate of advancement of the productive powers of labor is most efficiently promoted by no other policy of practice.

Article 4
International Monetary Policy

The only equitable and workable relations in financing of world trade among sovereign states with different economic and social systems is a system of credit based on fixed parities of national currencies, parities fixed by aid of a gold-reserve monetary order among states.

To prevent a gold-reserve system of fixed parities from becoming subject to disabling inflationary spirals, it is necessary to limit the extension of credit within the monetary system to "hard-commodity" categories of lending for import and export of physical goods. If such world trade emphasizes high proportions of efficiently employed advanced-technology capital-goods, the increase of productivity fostered by such trade has a secularly deflationary impact on prices.

In the present situation, in which world trade has been collapsing under pressures caused by pyramiding of refinanced external and domestic indebtedness of na-

tional economies, it is necessary to reorganize the present indebtedness, to the effect that low interest rates prevail in the anti-inflationary environment of a gold-reserve system, and that the schedule of repayments of existing, outstanding indebtedness does not consume more than 20% of the export earnings of any of these nations.

The general benefit of such monetary reforms is the creation, immediately, of greatly increased markets for trade in high-technology capital goods.

Article 5
Military Doctrines

Since the rupture of the wartime alliance between the two powers, U.S. military policy toward the Soviet Union has passed through two phases. The first, from the close of the war until a point beyond the death of Joseph Stalin, was preparation for the contingency of what was sometimes named "preventive nuclear war." The second, emerging over the period from the death of Stalin into the early period of the administration of President John F. Kennedy, was based on the doctrines of Nuclear Deterrence and Flexible Response as those doctrines were described in the keynote address by Dr. Leo Szilard at the second Pugwash Conference assembled in Quebec during 1958.

Until President Ronald Reagan's March 23, 1983 announcement of a new U.S. strategic doctrine, which overthrew the Nuclear Deterrence doctrine, from the time of the Kennedy administration, U.S. military doctrine toward the Soviet Union was more or less exactly that outlined by Szilard's keynote address at the second Pugwash Conference, of 1958. During the same interval, military negotiations between the Soviet Union and the U.S.A. have been premised on the assumption of continued U.S.A. adherence to the Nuclear Deterrence and Flexible Response doctrines.

From approximately 1963 until approximately 1977, it might have appeared, as it appeared to many, that the doctrines of Nuclear Deterrence and Flexible Response had succeeded in preserving a state of restive peace, something called "détente," between the two powers. This appearance was deceptive; during the period 1977-83, there was an accelerating deterioration in the military relationships between the two powers.

From the side of the United States, the impending breakdown of "détente" was signaled by the 1974 announcement of the so-called Schlesinger Doctrine. In fact, the Schlesinger Doctrine's perspective of "limited nuclear warfare" between the powers, or their so-called surrogates, was neither a violation of the Pugwash Doctrine, nor any innovation within that doctrine. Szilard, in outlining the doctrine in 1958, had already specified that the doctrine required provision for "limited nuclear warfare," as well as "local warfare" of a colonial-warfare variety.

The Schlesinger Doctrine's appearance was an embedded feature of Nuclear Deterrence and Flexible Response from the outset. If the Nuclear Deterrence doctrine were continued, it was already evident from the time of Szilard's 1958 address, "limited nuclear war" in the European theater was more or less an inevitable outcome.

Beginning shortly after the inauguration of President Jimmy Carter, the deterioration of the military situation accelerated. The Soviet Union's response was typified by the deployment of the SS-20 missiles in Europe, and the 1979 NATO response, prompted by Henry A. Kissinger, to deploy Pershing II and land-based cruise missiles as weapons to be deployed in an effort to induce the Soviet Union to eliminate the SS-20s deployment: the so-called double-track arms negotiations tactic.

As an arms-negotiation tactic, Kissinger's double-track gambit proved substantially less than worthless. Over the interval 1981-83, continuation of the Nuclear Deterrence/Flexible Response doctrine impelled both powers to the verge of the military postures of "Launch Under Attack" and the more ominous posture of "Launch On Warning."

In response to this direction of developments, the U.S. public figure Lyndon H. LaRouche, Jr. proposed that both powers develop, deploy, and agree to develop and deploy "strategic" defensive, anti-ballistic-missile defense based on "new physical principles." This proposal was issued publicly by LaRouche beginning February 1982; he proposed to U.S.A., Western European, and Soviet representatives that the development and deployment of such strategic defensive systems be adopted policy, as a means for escaping from the "logic" of Nuclear Deterrence.

During a period of not later than the 1962 appearance of Marshal V.D. Sokolovsky's *Military Strategy*, leading Soviet circles had recognized the dangerous fallacies of Nuclear Deterrence/Flexible Response doctrine from a military vantage-point, although no comparable assessment appeared as part of U.S.A. military doctrine until President Reagan's announcement of March 23, 1983.

In that sense, LaRouche's proposed strategic doctrine, as first announced publicly in February 1982, was congruent with the analysis first publicly offered by Marshal Sokolovsky in 1962. LaRouche's, and later, Dr. Edward Teller's and President Reagan's proposal of "Mutually Assured Survival," implicitly put both powers on the footing of identical military doctrines: LaRouche's doctrine, and President Reagan's, are properly judged to be U.S. versions of the Sokolovsky doctrine.

The leading objections raised, first, against LaRouche's proposal, and, later, the similar proposals of Dr. Teller and President Reagan, centered upon the observation that abandonment of Nuclear Deterrence/Flexible Response implied a new technological arms race centered around the development of layered ballistic missile defense. Examining the fallacy of that objection points toward the necessary changes in the military policy governing relevant negotiations between the two powers.

As key architects of Nuclear Deterrence, notably Bertrand Russell and Leo Szilard, emphasized most strongly during the 1950s and later, their purpose in proposing Nuclear Deterrence was to further Russell's feudalistic, utopian dream of creating an agency of world-government which would enjoy a monopoly of use and possession of means of warfare, including a monopoly of nuclear arsenals. Given the reality of Soviet development of nuclear arsenals, Russell et al. abandoned their earlier policy of "preventive nuclear warfare." They proposed to divide the world, at least temporarily, between what were proposed to be in effect, two world empires, an eastern and western division of the world between two "empires."

Nuclear Deterrence and Flexible Response were presented by Russell et al. as means for making general thermonuclear warfare between the two principal powers "unthinkable." The ability of either power to assure the annihilation of the other was argued to represent physical means for ensuring the preservation of the "two-empire" system. Flexible Response was added, to provide means for military adjustments, including local, and limited-nuclear warfare, without risking the escalation of such wars to general thermonuclear warfare.

History shows that such schemes are inherently unworkable. Exemplary is the case of the plan to divide

EIRNS/Stuart Lewis

Lyndon LaRouche speaking at a Directed Energy Beam Weapons Defense Technologies conference in Washington, D.C., April 13, 1983.

the Persian Empire into two parts, Eastern and Western Divisions, during the fourth century B.C. Also exemplary is the effort of the Venice-centered European "black nobility" to orchestrate balance of power among the Ottoman, Austro-Hungarian, Russian, and German empires, during the interval 1453-1914 A.D. The very logic of such attempted arrangements ensures wars leading to the destruction of one or all of the contending powers. Such is proving to be the case for the doctrines of Nuclear Deterrence and Flexible Response, respecting the deteriorating situation between the Atlantic and Warsaw Pact alliances.

It is the nature of competently elaborated military capabilities of major powers that those capabilities must be developed and prepared to ensure the survival and victory of the power in case of war with the opposing power. At the point that continuation of the existing form of peace is perceived to ensure the destruction of one of the powers, that power must either launch war or must accept the destruction of the nation which it repre-

sents. Marshal Sokolovsky and his Soviet co-thinkers were obviously correct on this point, and so was LaRouche.

The Nuclear Deterrence and Flexible Response doctrines were worse than merely incompetent. Had the threat of general warfare been perceived during the period beginning 1961-63, as Nuclear Deterrence seemed temporarily to remove that possibility, the powers would have been impelled to seek political and economic alternatives to such threats of general warfare. Instead, the political and economic impulses leading in the direction of warfare were permitted to aggregate. The political and economic impulses toward warfare were offset by adjustments in Nuclear Deterrence postures: including adjustments under the titles of détente generally, and arms-control agreements more narrowly. The unresolved political and economic issues seized upon the embedded logic of Nuclear Deterrence, to drive the powers to the verge of thermonuclear, general warfare.

The assumption prevailed, that as long as political and economic impulses toward general warfare did not surpass the "threshold" of Nuclear Deterrence, that such impulses toward war could be confidently maintained in existence, since neither power, it was assumed, would "dare to resort to the unthinkable" remedy of general thermonuclear warfare. So, under instruction of such deluded confidence in Nuclear Deterrence, the powers marched blindly toward the brink of general thermonuclear warfare.

If both powers and their allies were to deploy simultaneously the "strategic" and "tactical" defensive systems implicit in "new physical principles," the abrupt shift to overwhelming advantage of the defense would raise qualitatively the level of threshold for general warfare. This would be the case if defensive systems based on such "new physical principles" effectively deployed into the potential battlefield of Europe, as well as in the form of "strategic" defensive systems. For a significant period of time, the defense would enjoy approximately an order of magnitude of superiority, man for man, over the offense, relative to the previous state of affairs.

This would permit negotiation of a temporary solution to the imminence of a "Launch On Warning" posture by both powers: a solution which might persist for 10, 15 years, or longer. The true solution must be found in the domain of politics and economics, and the further shaping of military relations between the powers must produce military policies by each coherent with the direction of development of the needed political and economic solutions.

Articles 1-4 of this memorandum stipulate the leading, principled features of the required political and economic solutions. If each of the powers adheres to the republican military traditions exemplified by the work of Lazare Carnot and the Stein-Hardenberg reforms in Prussia, and defines its national interests according to the provisions of Articles 1-4, there need be no expectation of warfare between the powers: as warfare is the "continuation of politics by other means."

On the part of the United States of America, the government is committed to avoiding all colonial, imperial, or kindred endeavors in foreign policy, and to establish, instead, a growing community of principle among fully sovereign nation-states of this planet. This shall become a community of principle coherent with the policies of the articles of this draft memorandum. If any force should endeavor to destroy that community of principle, or any member of that community of sovereign nations, the United States will be prepared to defend that community and its members by means of warfare, should other means prove insufficient. With respect to the Soviet Union, the government of the United States offers the Soviet Union cooperation with itself in service of these principles, and desires that the Soviet Union might enter fully into participation within that community of principle.

Article 6
Weapons Policies of the Powers

The distinguishing kernel of most of the defensive weapons systems classed under the title of "new physical principles" is the development of applications of both accomplished and imminent breakthroughs in two of the three general areas of scientific progress to dominate the coming 50 years: controlled, high-energy plasmas, and directed-energy applications. The development of these military applications signifies an expansion of the varieties of research and development facilities and staffs occupied with such new technologies. The deployment of weapons systems of this class signifies development of production facilities oriented to these technologies.

The impact of this upon the economies is suggested by the reasonable estimate, that the U.S.A., Western Europe, Japan, and the nations of the Warsaw Pact, will spend aggregately about 1983 $3 trillion on development of "strategic" and "tactical" systems of this class by approximately the close of the present century, using U.S.A. costs as a standard of estimate. Although this amount is only a large ration of present levels of military expenditures by the same aggregation of states, to concentrate so large a ration of those military allotments upon the frontiers of present science and technology must have a very great impact upon the economies.

The best standard of comparison for estimating the impact of this upon the economies affected is the case of the impact of NASA research and development upon the U.S.A. economy, notably NASA's phase of intense development through 1966. The impact of the indicated program of high-technology military expenditures would be four to ten times as great as the NASA expenditure of that indicated period.

The impact of these technologies upon the civilian economies is suggested by the fact that the "second generation" of "commercial" fusion power might provide us with energy-flux densities in the order of as much as a half-million kilowatts per square meter, in contrast to between 40,000 and 70,000 kilowatts per square meter with best generating modes today. The industrial applications of high-powered lasers, including the important class of "tunable" such lasers, mean leaps in productive powers of labor, reasonably estimated to be as much as a twofold or threefold increase in productivity of U.S. operatives by the year 2000 A.D.

If this connection between military expenditures and civilian benefits is adequately realized, the return to society for such military expenditures will be many times the amount of the military expenditure.

Two conditions must be fulfilled.

First, it must be policy that new such technologies developed in the military area be rapidly introduced into the civilian area.

Second, the rate at which economies can assimilate new technologies is limited by the relative scale of and rate of capital turnover within the capital-goods sector of production, most emphatically within the machine-tool-grade sub-sector of capital-goods production.

The second of these conditions can not be adequately fulfilled unless the trend toward "post-industrial society," of the past 18 years, is sharply reversed. Although such an urgent change in policy of practice is chiefly a matter of domestic policy of sovereign nation-states, no sovereign nation-state can adequately pursue the needed policy-changes without very significant degrees of international cooperation.

To accomplish such a shift within sovereign states' economies, priorities must be set accordingly for investment allocations, in priorities for flows of credit, in relative costs of borrowing by priority categories of investment and employment, and in relative rates of taxation. Similar measures are required in international lending, including relative amounts available for financing international trade, and related extension of credit for investments of importing nations.

It should be general policy, that the goal for employment of operatives in agriculture, mining and refining, industrial production of physical goods, and as operatives developing and maintaining basic economic infrastructure ought to be not less than 50% of the total labor force of nations, and that employment for science and for research and development ought to be not less than 5% of the total labor force of nations. It should be general policy that the percentile of the total labor force employed as operatives in production of consumer goods ought not to increase, but that the increase in supply of consumer goods per capita should be fostered by high rates of capital investment per operative in such categories of production. In this way, the percentile of the operatives employed in capital-goods production should rise—assuming that not less than 50% of the labor forces are employed as operatives.

Under these conditions, provided that all nations share in development of the frontiers of scientific research, in laboratories, and in educational institutions, all nations will be made capable of assimilating efficiently the technological by-product benefits of the military expenditures on systems derived from application of "new physical principles."

To lend force to this policy, the powers agree to establish new institutions of cooperation between themselves and other nations in development of these new areas of scientific breakthrough for application to exploration of space.

To this purpose, the powers agree to establish at the earliest possible time institutions for cooperation in scientific exploration of space, and to also co-sponsor treaty-agreements protecting national and multinational programs for colonization of the Moon and Mars.

At some early time, the powers shall enter into deliberations, selecting dates for initial manned colonization of the Moon and Mars, and the establishment of international space stations on the Moon and in the orbits of Moon and Mars, stations to be maintained by and in the common interest and use of space parties of all nations.

The powers jointly agree upon the adoption of two tasks as the common interest of mankind, as well as the specific interest of each of the two powers: 1) The establishment of full economic equity respecting the conditions of individual life in all nations of this planet during a period of not more than 50 years; 2) Man's exploration and colonization of nearby space as the continuing common objective and interest of mankind during and beyond the completion of the first task. The adoption of these two working-goals as the common task and respective interest in common of the two powers and other cooperating nations, constitutes the central point of reference for erosion of the potential political and economic causes of warfare between the powers.

Article 7
Arms Negotiations Policy

The pre-existing arms-control treaties and related agreements between the two powers are to be superseded by new agreements consistent with the preceding Articles of this draft memorandum.

The existing and future arsenals of so-called "strategic" thermonuclear weapons are to be destroyed as rapidly as deployment of "strategic" defensive weapons systems renders such thermonuclear weapons technologically obsolete as weapons for general assault for general warfare.

On condition that such agreements sought progress as presently anticipated, the powers shall act first to withdraw all thermonuclear weapons in excess of some specific kilotonnage from territories of nations other than their own.

No arms agreement shall be sought whose verfiable adherence requires on-site inspection by personnel of a foreign nation. Rather, both powers and other nations shall be encouraged to deploy such methods of defense by aid of weapons-systems based on new physical principles, that any "cheating" in deploying weapons of assault is virtually nullified by capabilities of the defense.

Progress in implementing the agreements on policy identified in this draft memorandum shall be the precondition for negotiating additional agreements as may be deemed desirable.

TIME FOR HENRY C. CAREY, NOT HARAKIRI

The Forgotten Legacy of Tsuyoshi Inukai

by Asuka Burke

This article was composed in 2015-16.

At the beginning of the last century, Sun Yat-sen (1866-1925) and Tsuyoshi Inukai[1] (1855-1932) jointly embarked on a mission to introduce the American System of political economy to Asia. While Sun's idea has seen its blossoming today with President Xi's Belt and Road Initiative, in Japan, Inukai's legacy is almost lost in oblivion. That contrast is not a mere difference in economic policy—it is fundamental.

The following report[2] will uncover a shared history of Japan, China, and implicitly the United States, through the life of Tsuyoshi Inukai, to rediscover an idea that once united the three, and could, once again, unite them.

Bibliotheque Nationale de France

Japanese Prime Minister Inukai Tsuyoshi (seated center) with members of his cabinet in December, 1931.

1932

To better situate the life of Inukai, let us first start with the year 1932, a turning point in world history. In the United States, despite major opposition from the Wall Street faction inside the Democratic Party, Franklin D. Roosevelt won the presidential election, paving the way for a "New Deal" in America. Here was a light at the end of a long tunnel. At the same time, though unbeknownst to many, a similar situation existed on the other side of the Pacific: In Japan, Tsuyoshi Inukai, a student of the American System economist Henry C. Carey, won the prime ministership in the early Spring of 1932. His policy for the new administration was centered on two key issues: first, ending the Japanese invasion of Manchuria, and, second, launching an economic recovery based on a federal industrialization program not unlike FDR's New Deal. With Inukai in office, a potential existed for Japan to turn itself away from fascism, and, instead, rebuild its economy in the aftermath

---

1. Inukai is also known as Ki Inukai. His pen name, Mokudo, was taken from Laozi's teaching: "military strength leads the nation to its ruin, as a strong wood will be knocked down."

2. The research is dedicated to, and owes much to Mark Calney, who first uncovered the Inukai network and inspired this author to continue his unfinished work.

of the global depression. What would have been the course of world history if New Deal policies had been implemented on both sides of the Pacific?

On May 15, 1932, merely two months into his term in office, Inukai was assassinated by a dozen Japanese Imperial Army officers. Conspicuously, the Japanese media at that time was rather quiet about the murder of the Prime Minister, and the sentences against the offenders were so lenient that some among them were released, and assassinated again. From the time of this violent coup until the end of World War II, military generals dominated the office of Prime Minister and the cabinet.

To this day, explanations of Inukai's death as a mere "incident" have been accepted and tolerated. Yet his *life* attests to the contrary; for the British Empire to initiate "the Great Pacific War," his death was a *sine qua non*.

Inukai Tsuyoshi

Henry C. Carey and Tsuyoshi Inukai

Born in 1855, Tsuyoshi Inukai grew up at the time of a great transformation in Japan. For 200 years, under the rule of the Tokugawa shogunate, Japan had closed its door to the rest of the world, limiting its external trade to the Dutch trading post on an artificial island in Nagasaki. That was broken suddenly in 1854 with the opening up of its ports by U.S. Commodore Perry. The Meiji Restoration that followed, united the nation under the Emperor system. The new era was marked by intellectual curiosity for the world outside, as was exemplified by the Iwakura Mission of 1871, in which the entire Japanese cabinet, including Prime Minister Iwakura, left the country for a two-year world tour, to learn from governments abroad. The mission traveled to the United States, Britain, Germany, Russia, Egypt, Singapore, China, and other countries. The new ideas brought back from abroad, in turn, set off extensive policy debates among the intelligentsia in Japan. What economic policy is best suited for the new nation? How should the nation trade with others? What currency system should the nation employ?

There were more questions than answers, but one of

the epicenters of that policy debate was the American System of political economy versus British free trade doctrine. The American System is characterized by the issuing of national credit for infrastructure and protective tariffs to support national industry. For the champion of the American System at that time, Henry C. Carey, the difference was not merely one of policy. The American System was a flagship operation to prove to the world that the productive potential of labor could be harnessed to elevate the condition of all men—such that humanity might eradicate "the detestable system known as the Malthusian [doctrine], … thus vindicating the policy of God to man."[3] The successful industrialization of America's northern states, in the midst of the U.S. Civil War, attests to the validity of Carey's economic policies, as implemented under the Lincoln Administration.

Two members of the Iwakura Mission, Tetsunosuke Tomita and Norikazu Wakayama, in particular, played key roles in promoting the American System in Japan.[4] Tomita met with Henry C. Carey in Philadelphia in 1875. To his visitor from the Far East, Carey gave a sharp warning: "to tell you one thing: Do not trust any white man

---

3. "…to prove that among the people of the world, whether agriculturists, manufacturers, or merchants, there is perfect harmony of interests, and that the happiness of individuals, as well as the grandeur of nations, is to be promoted by perfect obedience to that greatest of all commands, 'Do unto others as ye would that others should do unto you'—is the object and will be the result of that mission. Whether that result shall be speedily attained, or whether it shall be postponed to a distant period, will depend greatly upon the men who are charged with the performance of the duties of government. If their movements be governed by that enlightened self-interest which induces man to seek his happiness in the promotion of that of his fellow-man, it will come soon. If, on the contrary, they be governed by that ignorant selfishness which leads to the belief that individuals, party, or national interests are to be promoted by measures tending to the deterioration of the condition of others, it will be late." Henry C. Carey, *The Harmony of Interests,* 1864.
4. Wakayama was an advocate for a social security system and started the first life insurance corporation in Japan, which later became known as Meiji Seimei. In 1878, he translated John Byles' *Sophisms of Free-Trade.*

without reason. Look at how certain white men colonized India, and what these people are now exporting to China. Who is exploiting all the resources in India? Who is bringing opium into China and addicting millions? Which nationality of people are planning to trample down Asia, and spread their menacing effects elsewhere? These are the questions you should ask."

Carey then warned that the free-trade doctrine is

neither for the benefit of your nation nor for the happiness of your citizens, rather it is like drinking very strong and poisonous vodka.

At the end of the meeting, Carey gave Tomita his economics book, and asked him to translate it into Japanese.

Soon after the Iwakura Mission returned home, Tomita became the second Governor of the Bank of Japan, and Wakayama became the first advocate for the national pension system, modeled upon that of German Chancellor Bismarck. Despite their busy schedules, however, they did not fail to find a brilliant young economist best suited for the translation: Tsuyoshi Inukai.

The young Inukai was a virtual nobody until, at the age of 25, he founded the *Tokai Economic Newspaper*, for the promotion of protectionism, in outright opposition to the *Tokyo Economic Magazine*,[5] a loud promoter of the free-trade doctrine. This student of Yukichi Fukuzawa[6] at Keio, well versed in Western economic theo-

Henry C. Carey

ries including the works of Mathew Carey's network, competently battered the authorities of the free-trade doctrine, not hesitating to call them out by name.

Recognizing his potential, Wakayama and Tomita lent aid to Inukai in his fight against the *Tokyo Economic Magazine*. Serving as a mentor, Wakayama gave Inukai all the books he had on American System economics, and he suggested that Inukai translate Henry C. Carey's *Principles of Social Science*. Tomita, for his part, wrote an introduction to the book, in which he recounted Carey's warning as quoted above. Thus, in 1884, Inukai's translation of Carey's *Principles of Social Science* was published by the Japanese Ministry of Finance.

Five years after the publication of Carey's book, Wakayama and Tomita organized the publishing of *The National System of Political Economy* by Friedrich List, the brilliant German promoter of American System economics. The translator of the work, economist Sadamatsu Oshima, consequently became known as the "Friedrich List of Japan." Still to this day, the name Friedrich List appears in Japanese public school textbooks as an opponent of Adam Smith's free trade doctrine.

For Inukai, his work on the American System during his career running the *Tokai Economic Newspaper* forged a solid foundation for the policy outlook which guided his political life as a member of the Diet, beginning in 1890.

Inukai as a Politician

Sangyo Rikkoku (industrialism) was Inukai's consistent policy throughout the 40-odd years of his politi-

---

5. The magazine, founded in 1879 by Ukichi Taguchi, was modeled on *The Economist*. Eisaku Ishikawa, translator of Adam Smith's *The Wealth Of Nations*, served as its lead editor.

6. Fukuzawa (1835-1901) was the intellectual leader of the Meiji Restoration. During the 1840s and 1850s, he was a member of the Dutch Studies movement, a group of young intellectuals who flocked to the Dutch colony at Nagasaki, the only venue for the study of Western science during the Edo period. He became a founder of Keio University,

the first university in Japan, where American professors from the school of Henry Carey and Mathew Carey lectured.

cal life.[7] As Japan lacked resources and land area, he saw it necessary to focus on increasing the productive powers of labor, which he identified as "an immaterial, yet highest form of wealth." The issuing of treasury bills "to develop science, improve technology, and organize a better transportation system," was therefore indispensable.

Sangyo Rikkoku was a crucial factor to stop the idea of needing military invasions of other nations to obtain resources. At the end of World War I, Inukai made a daring proposal to drastically reduce the military budget by slashing in half the number of army divisions, closing down military elementary schools, and bringing back all the Japanese forces stationed in China. The resources saved, Inukai further proposed, should be used for the industrialization and cultural progress of the nation. The proposal so outraged military commanders that they never forgave Inukai.

At the center of his policy of *Sangyo Rikkoku* was the establishment of the Academy of Science, modeled upon that of Germany. While such an academy had existed in Japan since 1917, it was a privately funded small-scale research center. Inukai called for an upgraded national academy, fully financed by the government, with branches established in all prefectures. He imagined an academy powerful enough to fuel the entire Japanese economy with the highest level of technology possible. He also saw such an academy as providing solutions to the utter failure of the educational system at that time. Instead of raising youth with moral principle, Inukai once lamented, the rampant liberalism of the day produced adults who were "as spiritless as a sea cucumber."

Besides his commitment to the American System, what drove Inukai as a politician was Confucianism. Jiro Hoshijima, Inukai's former secretary, sent a letter to Inukai in 1917, the year of Hoshijima's first election to the Diet, asking him what it means to be a good politician. Hoshijima, who later implemented Inukai's policy as Minister of Industry and Commerce in the first civilian government after World War II, never forgot what Inukai wrote back to him:

There is nothing special about becoming a pol-

Calligraphy of a Confucian teaching.

itician, since to be a politician is nothing but to be a human. Unlike other businesses, however, your objective is not your personal gain, but the interest of the whole nation, and of humanity, to which you must be completely dedicated.

Inukai continued:

… It was said that at the age of 70, Confucius followed his heart's desire without breaking moral principles. I wonder when I myself would be able to gain such a degree of freedom, as there is still a long way to go. Yet, if you ask me what it means to be a politician, that would be my answer. That is the principle.

Unlike his predecessor Yukichi Fukuzawa, Inukai never left Confucianism for the sake of Western ideals. For him, the notion of *"agapē"* in Christianity coincided with the Confucian notion of *"jin."* In 1929, Inukai visited Confucius's hometown, Qufu, China, with the hope of creating a Confucius university there. A strong sense of humanism, fostered by Confucianism and the American System, was at the heart of Inukai's economic policies, a characteristic that made him an enemy of the British Empire.

Abraham Lincoln Meets Henry C. Carey

Across the ocean, in Hawaii, there was a young Chinese revolutionary committed to the realization of the American System: Sun Yat-sen. Educated in Hawaii by American missionaries of the Benjamin Franklin

---

7. This was so in spite of the fact that he changed party eight times, often leaving one out of disgust for its corruption, to start a new one.

tradition,[8] young Sun became familiar with Western medicine, the republican form of government, and Christianity, in which he was baptized. Particularly influential in Sun's development as a revolutionary was Abraham Lincoln. Sun's "Three Principles of the People," Nationalism, Democracy, and People's Livelihood, were explicitly modeled upon Lincoln's Gettysburg Address: "government of the people, by the people, for the people." Moreover, Sun saw America's republican form of government as the solution to colonialism in Asia, as he realized that the same British strategy that had been used to divide the United States, was now being deployed against China. In Sun Yat-sen's 1912 appeal "To the Friends of China in the United States of America," he wrote:

Sun Yat-sen in London, 1896.

We understand too well that there are certain men of power—not to include for the present, certain nations—who would view with a greater or lesser satisfaction an internal rupture in the new Republic [of China]. They would welcome, as a move toward the accomplishment of their own ends and designs, a civil war between the provinces of the North and the South; just as, 50 years ago, there was applause in secret (in certain quarters) over the terrible civil strife in the United States.

Had the war been successful from the South's standpoint, and had two separate republics been established, is it not likely that perhaps half a dozen or more weak nations would have eventually been established? I believe that such would have been the result; and I further believe that with the one great nation divided politically and commercially, outsiders would have stepped in sooner or later and made of America their own. I do not believe that I am stating this too forcibly.

If so, I have not read history nor studied men and nations intelligently. And I feel that we have such enemies abroad as the American republic had; and that at certain capitals the most welcome announcement that would be made would be that of a rebellion in China against the constituted authorities.

Thus, once Inukai had come to the forefront of the Japanese political scene, it was only a matter of time before the two revolutionaries found each other. Around 1897, Inukai employed Toten Miyazaki[9] as a secret agent tasked with finding pearls among Chinese revolutionaries who might become collaborators. To Miyazaki's surprise, he found the best of such pearls in his own backyard: After the failure of the Waichow revolt, Sun Yat-sen arrived in Yokohama, Japan. Sun, as a Chinese revolutionary, was already well-known through the earlier publication of his semi-autobiographical *Kidnapped in London,* a true story of Sun's capture in London by a Chinese legation, who, after getting Sun drunk, tried to smuggle him back to China to be executed, as the government had placed a price on Sun's head.

Once having met with Sun in Yokohama, Miyazaki wasted no time bringing "the living example" to Inukai. As expected, Sun and Inukai found a congenial spirit in each other at the very first meeting. Inukai was so impressed by Sun that he immediately pledged his support for Sun's revolution. He furnished him with a house in Tokyo, and took him to meet with leading politicians, including then Foreign Minister Shigenobu Okuma.[10]

---

8. Robert Wesser and Mark Calney, "Sun Yat-sen's Legacy and The American Revolution," *EIR,* Oct. 28, 2011.

9. Young Miyazaki first converted to Christianity and learned English. Soon disillusioned, however, he turned to Pan-Asianism, and traveled across China and South East Asia. All the while, he gained his fame in Japan as a singer of Rokyoku, traditional Japanese narrative singing. Later, he became an author of Sun's biography *33-year Dream.*

10. Inukai's house became a shelter for other prominent Asian revolutionaries of his time, such as Sun's protégés, Chiang Kai-shek, Kim Ok-gyun of Korea, and Rashbehari Bose of India.

Sun Yat-sen with friends in Tokyo, 1900.

Through these meetings, Sun recruited Japanese industrialists to finance his revolution. One such financier loved Sun's revolution so much, that after exhausting almost all of his resources, he went so deeply into debt to support the revolution that he had a six-month-long nervous breakdown!

The First Venture

Inukai and Sun's first joint project was to aid the Philippines independence movement led by Emilio Aguinaldo. As this was right after the 1894 Sino-Japanese war, they decided it would be better to win a republic in the Philippines first, to open up a better opportunity for creating a republic in China. Sun, Inukai, and Miyazaki quickly organized six million rounds of ammunition, ten thousand rifles, ten field guns, a pressing machine for gunpowder, one fixed cannon, and a dozen Japanese military experts to be sent, through Taiwan, to the Philippines.

However, their enterprise came to a sudden halt when the ship, overloaded with weaponry, sank in a storm off the shore of Shanghai. Soon after, Aguinaldo was captured by General Arthur MacArthur, who convinced him to pledge allegiance to the United States. For Aguinaldo, now a prisoner of war, everything seemed lost. Yet, in an ironic turn of events, thirty-two years later, Aguinaldo's follower, Manuel Quezon, would fight side by side with Arthur MacArthur's own son for the Philippines republic. For the Japanese, Chinese, and Filipinos who participated in the planning, this first attempt, despite its utter failure, proved to be the basis for further collaboration among Asian countries for expelling colonialism.

The Revolution of 1911

In October 1911, Sun's network in Wuchang staged a successful uprising against the Qing Dynasty. Sun and his military adviser Homer Lea hurriedly returned from the United States to score the final victory against the collapsing dynasty. Notably, on their way, they made a quick stop in Europe to arrange a deal that would prevent the Hong Kong & Shanghai Bank (HSBC) and J.P. Morgan from supplying loans to the Qing Dynasty through their newly formed "Consortium for China." By December of 1911, Inukai was in Shanghai to meet with Sun who embraced his old friend with tears in his eyes. The Revolution of 1911 successfully toppled the Qing Dynasty by early 1912, and established the Re-

Sun Yat-sen at a ceremony after the 1911 Revolution in China.

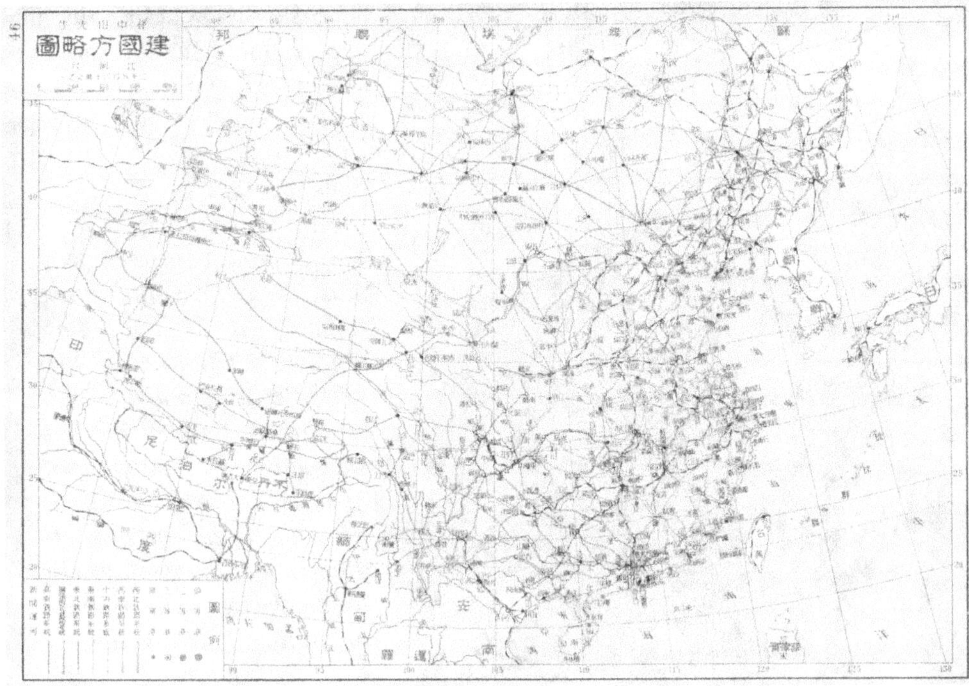

Sun Yat-sen's map for the development of China.

public of China with Sun as its provisional president.

In the midst of this success, Inukai warned of the British Empire's geopolitical manipulations. His apprehension was vindicated soon after the establishment of the Republic of China in 1912, when its new president, Yuan Shikai, expelled Sun's Nationalist party from the parliament and declared Yuan to be the Emperor! Thus by 1913, Sun had to call for a second revolution, this time against Yuan. Behind Yuan's audacity, of course, was significant financing from the HSBC-led "Five Power Banking Consortium," which enabled him to defy any opposition. In return for payment, the major powers proceeded with further divisions of China: "The 21 demands" of 1915 put several Chinese territories under Japan's sphere of influence, and the Versailles Treaty followed that up with further territorial gains by the major powers.

Yet, this was only a prelude to what was to come later. With Morgan's Thomas W. Lamont as its leading figure, the second Consortium for China unrepentantly financed Japan's imperial scheme to build the Southern Manchurian Railway throughout the 1920s, in the name of the "development" of China. Ironically, in 1931, the Japanese Imperial Army bombed the rail line they had built and blamed it on the Chinese. Under that false claim, Japan invaded Manchuria.

Sun was not the least bit naive about the Empire's machinations. With his publication of *The International Development of China* (1919), Sun made known his daring proposal to make China a new frontier for the world, by developing rail networks, ports, and new cities, all outside of London's Consortium. To this end, Sun recruited the U.S. emissary Paul Reinsch to create the Sino-International Construction Company to build the proposed rail system.

Sun's keen insight into the situation is expressed in the preface of the book:

As soon as Armistice was declared in the recent World War, I began to take up the study of the

Yuan Shikai (center) at swearing in ceremony as provisional President.

International Development of China, and to form programs accordingly. I was prompted to do so by the desire to contribute my humble part in the realization of world peace. China, a country possessing a territory of 4,289,000 square miles, a population of 400,000,000 people, and the richest mineral and agricultural resources in the world, is now a prey of militaristic and capitalistic powers—a greater bone of contention than the Balkan Peninsula. Unless the Chinese question can be settled peacefully, another world war greater and more terrible than the one just past will be inevitable.

The same concern about geopolitical manipulation against China prompted Sun, from the very beginning of the 1911 revolution, to repeatedly request that Inukai become a top advisor to Yuan Shikai. Inukai, however, turned that offer down, choosing to serve his term in office as a Japanese parliamentarian. For his part, Inukai did continue to pressure the Japanese government to support the 1911 revolution and diplomatically recognize the new Republic, but his efforts were to no avail. As Sun and Inukai both came to recognize, Japan's foreign policy had increasingly mirrored that of the British Empire, especially since the Anglo-Japanese alliance of 1902. That treaty stipulated that Japan and Britain would jointly "intervene" and defend their "special interests" in China and Korea, should there be any disturbance arising in either.

Sun Yatsen

"All under heaven is for the public," handwritten by Sun Yat-sen, 1924.

Still, Sun kept insisting that Japan should support the revolution, as he wrote in a letter to Inukai, who relayed the message to the government officials in 1923:

The Japanese government must recognize the utter failure of its foreign policy regarding China thus far, and offer its support for the revolution. If the revolution succeeds, the people of Vietnam, Burma, Nepal, Bhutan, even India, Afghanistan, and Malay will follow the example of China in gaining their sovereignty from the Empire. The Chinese revolution, therefore, can be a death sentence for European imperialism.

The Poisonous Vodka

During the latter half of the 1920s, the increasing influence of Thomas Lamont over Japan further aggravated its imperial tendency. In 1924, he single-handedly refinanced Japan's Russo-Japanese War debt, originally issued by London, for $150 million: the biggest foreign loan ever made up until that time. As Japan was hit by a catastrophic earthquake in the same year, Lamont, by disguising the loan as an earthquake relief measure, became known as the hero who saved Japan after the earthquake. He even took a national tour, during which he was met with overwhelming jubilation by the population. While gaining greater influence over Japan, Lamont generously encouraged Japan's imperial policies, such as building the Southern Manchurian Railway.

The situation turned even more gloomy. On March 12, 1925, Sun died of cancer. Two months later, Inukai hosted his memorial service in Japan, and shortly after, he suddenly announced his retirement from politics. Although he did not mention Sun's death as a cause of his retirement, the loss of a kindred spirit with whom he fought together for almost 30 years certainly had great bearing on his decision. As a telling sign of their close relationship, when Sun's grave was moved from Beijing to the capital, Nanjing, in 1929, Inukai was one of four chosen to carry the coffin, despite the declining Sino-Japanese relationship at the time. Among the thousands assembled for the funeral procession, Inukai held a place of honor next to Sun's protégé, Chiang Kai-shek. Their shared commitment, however, was best described by Sun himself in his *International Development of China:*

Library of Congress

Thomas W. Lamont, Jr. 1918.

The relationship between China and Japan is one of common existence, or extinction. Without Japan, there would be no China; without China, there would be no Japan. Under the principle of Pan-Asianism, Japan and China can together develop the natural resources in the West of the Pacific.

In 1931, when all glimmers of hope seemed to disappear after Sun's death, and that very choice of *common existence, or extinction* fell upon the hand of Inukai, he suddenly came back into the forefront of Japanese politics as a candidate for Prime Minister. Even though Inukai had nominally "retired," in reality, he remained a member of the Diet, as the voters of Okayama prefecture simply put his name on the ballot, without his consent, and kept electing him! Thus on Sept. 18, 1931, the day the Japanese Army invaded Manchuria, there could not have been a better politician than Inukai to resolve the situation. His determination was such that he put off his real retirement, and, instead, led a vigorous and successful campaign for Prime Minister.

His top policy priority was to resolve the Manchurian invasion. As he made it no secret, a rumor that Inukai was going to stop the invasion and fire 30 military officers of a radical faction became known among the top layers of the military. Two days after the formation of his administration, Inukai sent his secret agent Nagatomo Kayano, a friend of Sun, to China to seek a diplomatic solution for the situation. However, his secret letters were intercepted and leaked to the Imperial Army by his own secretary, Kaku Mori.

The second policy Inukai called for was the rapid industrialization of the nation, in opposition to the reigning policy of imperial colonization elsewhere. True to his word, Inukai appointed Korekiyo Takahashi,[11] an enemy of Thomas Lamont and a critic of the Manchurian invasion, as his Finance Minister. For his third major policy, he proposed a reform to rid, not only the political system, but also the people themselves of cor-

---

11. In 1867, Takahashi, still a youth, went to Oakland, California and learned English while working as a slave building the Transcontinental Railroad.

Inuki (far left) and Takahashi next to him.

ruption, identifying fascism as one such corruption. Anybody who listens to his campaign address in 1932 will rightly wonder what would have been the course of history if these policies had been implemented. Yet that is exactly the reason why he had to be eliminated.

On Sunday, May 15, 1932, a dozen armed officers of the Imperial Army broke into Inukai's house. They quickly found and surrounded the unarmed old man, who stood there fearlessly in the face of the imminent threat. "I understand, just don't push yourself so hard. Let us talk," said Inukai, and he invited them to his tea room for a dialogue. Caught off guard by Inukai's absolute calmness and unexpected hospitality, all the officers stood still for a moment, not knowing what to do. When one of them started to take off his shoes, as is customary, to go into the room, the leader of the assassins shouted at once: "There's no excuse! Shoot him!" The next moment, Inukai was shot. Even that was not enough to cause Inukai to lose his nerve. He told his son who had just rushed into the room: "That was such a short distance, and yet they've had only two hits (out of seven). ...So much for their military training!" Until his last breath later on that day, Inukai kept insisting: "Given a dialogue, they will understand."

What may not have been clear even to Inukai, however, is that he was killed by assassins who had no hatred against him. The trial proceedings of the offenders that took place soon after the assassination, show how the assassins were all controlled, if not literally brainwashed, from the top. Every single offender admitted that he had no animosity toward Inukai personally, and some even admired Inukai as a politician. Nevertheless, they mindlessly claimed that "he had to be killed for a higher end," as this was repeatedly said

Tsuyoshi Inukai at home.

by their masterminds, such as Shumei Okawa and Ikki Kita. The sentences given to the offenders were so lenient that some of them took part in other assassinations later. One of these was the coup of 1936, in which Kita was involved. In this, Inukai's Finance Minister, Korekiyo Takahashi, and his pro-American friend, Makoto Saito, then the Interior Minister, were brutally assassinated. Saito, nearly 80 years old, was shot by the dozens of young assassins so many times that doctors had to give up taking the bullets out of his body after removing 47 of them. This assassination further accelerated Japan's drive toward war because these two leaders were key collaborators of Joseph C. Grew, the American Ambassador to Japan, who sought to avoid the collision course with the United States until 1941. The brutal and numerous murders and assassination plots throughout the 1930s imposed a reign of terror, under which nobody dared to oppose the fascism that now wholly took over the nation. Tokyo sent radical fascists, including those who had participated in these assassinations, to China where their brutality fully exploded in the Nanjing Massacre of 1937.

It's the British!

To simply conclude that Inukai was killed by the radical faction of the Japanese military because he went against their imperial scheme, misses the point. At that time, fascism was promoted not only in Japan, but also in Germany, Italy and elsewhere simultaneously by Wall Street and London. This was an intentional push for a global fascism, aimed at the orchestration of a new world war. Inukai's assassination became an absolute necessity only within this context.

In 1925, the year Sun died, the British naval analyst Hector Bywater published a "fictional story," the novel titled *The Great Pacific War.* Using the latest and most accurate data available on the resources and capabilities of both Japan and the United States, Bywater developed a fictional account of a new world war that conspicuously matched the reality that was to unfold not long after the publication of the book.

The story begins with a "well-known New York banker" getting a concession to develop iron and coal fields in a region of China considered a territory of Japanese interest. Simultaneously, a mass rally of communists erupts in Japan over the deaths of civilian demonstrators and the arrest of one of the prominent communist leaders. Soon, the communists surround the parliament and a bomb targeting cabinet members is set off inside the building. Then, the Japanese government decides to use the attack by "the communists" as a pretext for establishing a dictatorship, with an eye to expanding its "sphere of influence" in China. In the name of defeating the financial interests behind China's militarism, Japan conducts a Pearl Harbor-style surprise attack against the United States, the Philippines, the Panama Canal and other places, and takes over Manchuria and other key strategic spots for their resources.

A war between Japan and the United States, the purportedly communist-led "Reichstag fire," the invasion of Manchuria, and the attack on Pearl Harbor had all been fully scripted by the British Navy, which trained the *crème de la crème* of the Japanese naval officers at the time.

Not only scripted, but also taught: The British provided Japan with intelligence on the British-led attack at the Battle of Taranto in 1940, which required a special technique to attack a target on shore surrounded by very shallow water, just like Pearl Harbor. The Japanese naval officers were even allowed to inspect the actual site of the battle to learn the technique, which was then transmitted to top Japanese generals.

Not only scripted and taught, but, most importantly, financed. Thomas Lamont's 1924 Second Consortium, which refinanced the war debt, and his financing of the *Zaibatsu*[12] faction whose money was then poured into the Manchurian invasion, fully fed and bred the Japanese Empire. It is obvious that the Japanese fascists, who were an extreme minority at the beginning of the 1930s, could not have been so successful were it not

for external support. This methodology was not limited just to Japan: fascism was promoted globally by London and Wall Street. While Lamont financed Japan's imperial expansion, he was at the same time handing out a $100 million loan to Mussolini, describing himself as "something like a missionary" for Italian fascism. Brown Brothers Harriman, Rockefeller's Standard Oil, and other prominent Wall Street firms similarly fostered fascism in Germany and elsewhere. The United States itself was not immune to such schemes. During the Democratic convention of 1932, Morgan banking interests, which owned a good chunk of the Democratic Party, led a massive campaign to get Roosevelt off the ballot. Though Roosevelt, by a slight margin, succeeded in winning the Democratic Party nomination, later—on Feb. 15, 1933—an assassination attempt was made against his life, right before his inauguration. And if that was not enough, within less than a year, the Morgans and the Du Ponts were caught plotting a military coup d'etat against the new Roosevelt administration. Major General Smedley Darlington Butler, who was approached by the Morgan agent Gerald MacGuire to lead an army of veterans, foiled the coup at the last minute by exposing the plot to the Congress.[13]

Though the full account of the British geopolitical manipulation is not the central subject of this current report, it is evident that the Empire had in mind "a higher end" for which the life of Inukai had to be terminated. Not only would Inukai's friendship with China have most certainly spoiled the Empire's scenario for war between Japan and America, but his familiarity with the American System of political economy could have brought about profound cooperation across the Pacific. The British Empire could not tolerate this outcome. Thus the course was set for the assassinations of Inukai and his circle, and, soon after, for the lives of more than sixty million souls to be violently terminated in the deadliest conflict ever known in human history.

A Spiritual Salvation: 1945

On the morning of Sept. 2, 1945, the butchery of World War II was brought to a close with the official armistice signed on the deck of the battleship *USS Missouri.* The Japanese delegation which attended the signing had written their wills to their families prior to

---

12. Industrial and financial business conglomerates in the Empire of Japan.

13. "Wall Street Backed The Plot To Kill FDR," *EIR*, Oct. 21, 2011.

General Douglas MacArthur (center) reads Japanese surrender terms on board USS Missouri in Tokyo Bay.

the event, as they expected that they would be executed by their former enemy on the spot. To their surprise, they were treated as diplomats of a sovereign nation. There was no violence, nor even a word of condemnation. General of the Army Douglas MacArthur's speech on the occasion exemplified the spirit of the time:

> Men since the beginning of time have sought peace. Various methods through the ages have been attempted to devise an international process to prevent or settle disputes between nations. From the very start, workable methods were found in so far as individual citizens were concerned, but the mechanics of an instrumentality of larger international scope have never been successful. Military alliances, balances of power, Leagues of Nations, all in turn failed, leaving the only path to be "by way of the crucible of war." The utter destructiveness of war now blocks out this alternative. We have had our last chance. If we will not devise some greater and more equitable system, Armageddon will be at our door. The problem basically is theological and involves a spiritual recrudescence and improvement of human character that will synchronize with our almost matchless advances in science, art, literature, and all the material and cultural developments of the past 2,000 years. It must be of the spirit, if we are to save the flesh.

> In reporting back the surrender ceremony to the Emperor, a member of the Japanese delegation made the honest reflection that Japan, if it had been victorious, would not have treated the former enemy with such magnanimity.

> After all, we were not beaten on the battlefield by dint of superior arms. We were defeated in the spiritual contest by virtue of a nobler idea. The real issue was moral—beyond all the powers of algebra to compute.

A Spiritual Salvation, Today

It is this spirit that separates present-day China from Japan and the nations of the trans-Atlantic region today. While some people in the latter group may viciously pursue rivalry with China over GDP, or military might, nevertheless, that very method of thinking—British imperial geopolitics—is no match for China's nobler idea, which "elevat[es] while equalizing the condition of man throughout the world," to borrow Henry C. Carey's words. A new global infrastructure network and ambitious national space programs including fusion research, are redefining the relationship of man and nature, ushering in the new era of mankind as a spacefaring species.

Is Japan ready to join with China in this "spiritual contest"? Or, will it remain the country of "spiritless sea cucumbers"? The answer is yet to be heard from those who represent today the daring spirit of Tsuyoshi Inukai. While his life was suddenly and violently terminated, his legacy lives on, and quietly awaits its revival.

Kesha Rogers on Explorer I Anniversary

by Stephanie Ezrol

Feb. 4—Kesha Rogers sent a video message to President Trump on Jan. 29 before his State of the Union address, highlighting the 60th anniversary of the first successful American satellite, Explorer 1, which was launched on Jan. 31, 1958. In a refreshing show of courage and honesty, and in a clearly bipartisan spirit, she called for rebuilding NASA's manned space program, putting an end to the British-empire-allied Wall Street predatory privatizers who lead "the outright intention to destroy our space program" using "budget cutters, privatizers, and radical so-called environmentalists pushing an anti-growth culture." She echoed space scientist Kraft Ehricke's profound message that "no one and nothing under the natural laws of the universe impose any limitation on man except man himself." When we say we are going to put limitations on the development of a full-fledged U.S. mission to a revived and renewed space program, "we are doing this to ourselves."

NASA/Joel Kowsky

National Academy of Sciences 60th Anniversary of the Explorer 1 mission and the discovery of Earth's Van Allen radiation belts. Thomas Zerbuchen, Associate Administrator for NASA's Science Mission Directorate.

Rogers is an independent candidate for Congress in Texas's 9th Congressional District. She became internationally famous in February 2014 when a University of Texas poll showed her to be the front-runner in the Democratic primary for the U.S. Senate. In 2010 and 2012, she won the Democratic nomination in the 22nd Congressional District on the program "Save NASA, Impeach Obama," without any organizational or financial backing from the Democratic Party.

The LaRouche Political Action Committee (LPAC), with whom she has aligned her current campaign, has called for implementing "LaRouche's Four Laws" and for joining China's great Belt and Road Initiative to "create millions of productive jobs, and ensure the United States joins a new paradigm of global collaboration on great infrastructure projects advancing the common aims of mankind."

All human progress is marked by a march into the unknown fueled by human creativity in tune with a creative universe. The 1958 mission is a good reminder of America's stellar role in that progress. "The small, pencil-shaped satellite did more than launch the U.S. into the Space Age. With its collection of instruments and scientific tools, it turned space into not just a new frontier, but also a place of boundless scientific exploration that could eventually unveil secrets of new worlds as well as the mysteries of our own planet," re-

JPL Director William Pickering, University of Iowa physicist James Van Allen, space scientist Wernher von Braun (shown left to right) holding a model of Explorer 1.

ports the NASA Jet Propulsion Laboratory at the California Institute of Technology on this 60th Anniversary.

James Van Allen led a team at the University of Iowa, which developed instruments to measure the concentration of ions and electrons in space to detect cosmic rays, the high-energy particles originating beyond the Solar System. Explorer 1 found more than cosmic rays. Following a revolutionary hypothesis of Dr. Van Allen, two concentric rings of high-energy particles circling the Earth were discovered, originating from the Sun. Those belts were later named for their discoverer.

The Challenge of Cosmic Radiation

That investigation of cosmic radiation has been a hallmark of the scientific genius of Lyndon LaRouche, the world's most successful economic forecaster since the end of World War II. LaRouche in a 2010 article, "The Secret Economy's Outlook," reprinted in last week's *EIR*, called for "A fresh definition of universal physical space-time, restating the intention of the Mendeleyev periodic table in terms of a universal system of cosmic radiation," as one of the four crucial elements of a principle of physical economy. Explorer 1 reminds us that the American commitment to move in that direction, in the minds of our most creative and courageous scientists, engineers, astronauts and political figures, has a long and proud history.

The now 95-year-old LaRouche in 2010 harkened back to the clear mission of President John Kennedy and his NASA collaborators, "Even before a likely manned landing on Mars, which may require preparations during several generations to come, we must come to grips with the reality, that there is 'no empty space' out there. Contrary to what might be wrongly considered to be some 'empty space' between the orbits of Earth and Mars, the illusion of the existence of 'empty space,' is to be recognized as what might be considered as the result of a 'planning failure' in the design of humanity's sense-organs.

"What is called 'space' is jammed-full of a mass of varieties of cosmic radiation. Thus, one of the tasks to be tackled beginning the very near future, is a certain degree of reorganization of the so-called 'periodic table' of physical chemistry, to reflect the implications of a space jammed full of cosmic radiation assorted into sundry sorts of variously 'hard' and 'soft' radiation flowing from and to assorted potential targets.

"This challenge has been expressed by the celebrated example of particle-wave paradoxes of the celebrated experiments of de Broglie and those who contributed to the matter of the broader implications of his discovery. The relevant evidence presents us the strong suggestion that the reading of the periodic table must be restated in terms of these considerations of 'wave functions' in the domain of cosmic radiation, as such a view is typified by Academician V.I. Vernadsky's partition of physical space-time among the

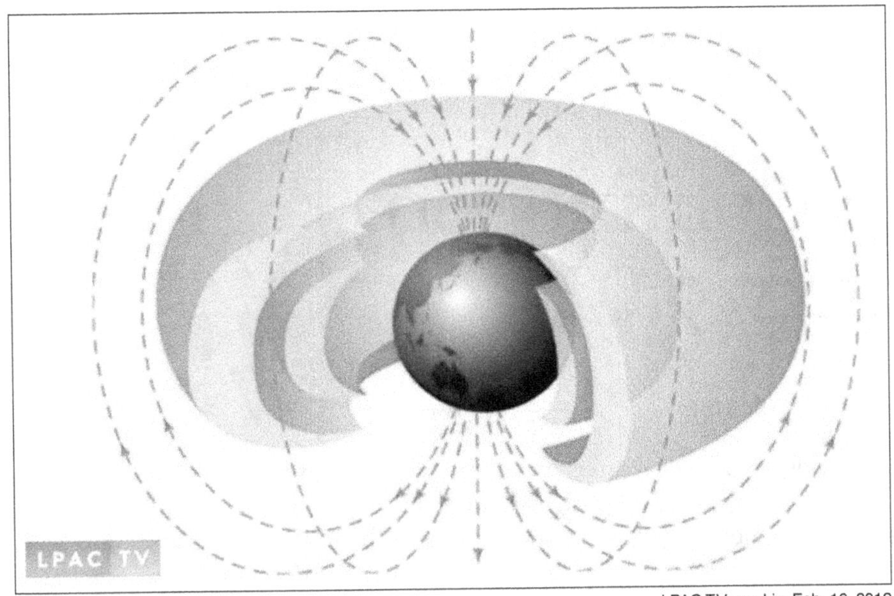

LPAC TV graphic, Feb. 16, 2012

The Van Allen Belts.

abiotic, the biosphere, and the noösphere."

On to an Unlimited Future in 2018

LPAC'S 2018 "Campaign to Win the Future" is a rallying cry for a future-oriented platform very much in tune with the new paradigm underlying China's Belt and Road Initiative and the hopes and aspirations of all of humankind for a science-driven pursuit of happiness and prosperity. At a July 31 National Academy of Science symposium, "A Celebration of the Explorer 1 Mission and the Discovery of Earth's Radiation Belts" Thomas Zurbuchen, associate administrator for NASA's Science Mision Directorate, described the recent discovery by the twin Van Allen probes of "a third belt, which is transitory" as a "a new part of nature that is something beautiful."

The insanity of the current McCarthyite Russiagate atmosphere in the United States was manifest in the denial of a visa to a Russian scientist who was invited to make a presentation of the lesser-known Russian research in radiation belt physics.

Despite such foolishness, the march of a hopeful new paradigm is clearly unstoppable. Think of the universal good of humankind pursuing a creative role off and on the planet as a New Silk Road in Space. Like John F. Kennedy, an earlier young, great American, Kesha Rogers emphasized, "A renewed mission in the American space program must be reaffirmed, for the good of humanity. No back channel, privatized, low ball, money deals. The time of saying 'been there, done that' has passed, and we must recommit ourselves to the inspiration and dedication of those great scientists and leaders who paved the way for us, 60 years ago today.

We must once again firmly re-establish our foothold in space with a renewed national mission to pick up where we left off, and go back to the Moon as the basis for further exploration and discovery. Our foothold in space is not going to be limited by budget cuts. We cannot say that we are going to put $19.1 billion into NASA and hope that this will be enough money, knowing that it won't. We need to go forward with a full commitment to the full-fledged development of mankind in space as a driver for alleviating poverty, an economic driver that's going to put everybody to work in productive jobs: this has to be a commitment without limitations."

Why So Much Commotion Around Industry 4.0?

by Andrea Andromidas

Everyone is talking about "Industrie 4.0," a purported new industrial revolution, about the Internet of Things, Big Data, cloud-computing and the worldwide networking of all of them. If this is really an industrial revolution, it would be interesting to know what it is.

People in manufacturing industries, who have been involved in the production of digital components or even robots for decades, undoubtedly have some idea of the direction further progress is expected to take, but they are baffled as to why there has been such a commotion around the above-mentioned subjects. Extensive reports on future production processes from the Fraunhofer Institute—Europe's largest application-oriented research organization— unfortunately do not focus on this theme, but are more concerned with the problem of volatile markets and other uncertainties. Moreover, no one can claim that the digitalization era is only beginning today, given the enormous development of digital manufacturing technology for decades now, including in other parts of the world, emphatically including Asia.

So why such a fuss about a German expression for which an English translation has not even been found? The head of Siemens, Jo Kaeser, in a Sept. 23, 2017 interview with *Spiegel*, hinted that the answer to this question is not to be found in the realm of industrial production, because it actually concerns a different kind of revolution:

Spiegel: Do traditional enterprises have enough innovative means and resiliency to call into question their own business model and to cannibalize it if need be?

Kaeser: That will be the vital question for the German economy. How fast will it be able to adapt in an uncertain environment, which is constantly changing and rapidly? … We are also really strong when it comes to integrating software into hardware. Now, we have to find our way to solution-oriented software business models.[1]

The explanation is given in a 2017 fact sheet from Bitkom, Germany's digital industry association. As a member of the platform Industrie 4.0, Bitkom conducted a survey of 559 large companies (100 or more employees) on the subject of Industrie 4.0, and released the results together with recommendations in a 30-page paper. It is stated right in the introduction that 69% of all those surveyed have a totally wrong assessment of Industrie 4.0, because they assume that it involves increased efficiency for existing industrial processes.

Only 14 % were right:

Only 14% are pursuing with Industrie 4.0 first and foremost the goal of developing new business models or changing existing business models. With such a prioritization, the German economy is threatened with falling behind sooner rather than later. As reality already shows, the

Josef Kaeser, CEO Siemens, AG.

---

1. http://www.spiegel.de/spiegel/joe-kaeser-ueber-digitalisation-schicksalsfrage-der-wirtschaft-s ein-a-1169382.html

actual revolution of Industrie 4.0 does not occur in production but in the business models. Of particular importance here are digital platforms. With their data-based value added services, they act as go-betweens between producer and client, severing the customary relations between them and thus posing a serious challenge to established enterprises. In the worst case, they will be reduced to exchangeable sub-contractors, while the digital platforms can take in the lion's share of the industrial value-added.[2]

On page 11, the following is said of the new notion of "Internet of Things":

In the course of digitalization, the archetype of a broker has gained significantly more attention through the emergence of so-called platform enterprises. These enterprises traditionally earn their money by bringing together suppliers and demanders, and charge a fee for their service, typically from the supplier. What is special about it, is that the entire transaction, from search to selection and then up to payment, takes place on a digital platform.

UBER, a success story?

The exemplary success stories ("disruptive game changers") that are cited not only in this work, but in all discussions of this kind, are the taxi company UBER, the lodgings broker Airbnb, Netflix, Google and Amazon.

The Energy Transition Serves as Testing Ground

In February 2017, a conference took place in Berlin, which was described by its organizer "Management Circle" as an exclusive meeting of executives in the energy industry. The title of the conference was: "The Reorientation of Energy Companies." The relevant documentation states that because of the well-established "energy transition," the decentralization of production, the Internet of things and the new demands on networks, digitalization plays a central role in the energy industry.

The report includes comments from Dr. Urban Keussen of TenneT, Alf Henryk Wulf of GE Power, and Dr. Marie-Luise Wolff-Hertwig of Entega. Other participants included Michael Feist of the Hanover municipal utility company, Dr. Luge of E.ON and Andreas Mundt from the Federal Cartel Office. Alf Henryk Wulf is reported to have said that GE wanted to use its PREDIX cloud platform to ultimately transform the corporation into a software company.

The presentation of Dr. Marie-Luise Wolff-Hertwig of Entega AG was reported to have been "groundbreaking." Her title was: "Does the Energy Branch Lack Digital Literacy?" The energy branch should be prepared, she said, to come up with entirely new service models, because digitalization is less a technical than a social task, and demands an entirely new business culture. A quote from the summary:

Management boards have to adjust to that, because a work culture in "granite," which is often still customary practice in Germany, where the "zero-error principle" prevails and processes are standardized down to the smallest—this work culture prevents enterprises from being innovative, trying out new things, changing. We should look to Silicon Valley more often, where things are much more in flux and frequent failures are accepted....

Every change on the market should be checked to see whether it could be made into a new service ... This sector talks too much about boilers, it is said, rather than making their products "sex" ... A basic attitude is needed that factors failure into business, and has the courage to take risks. Active entrepreneurship

---

2. Bitkom fact sheet from June 2017 titled: "Business models in Industrie 4.0, Using and Actively Helping to Shape Opportunities and Potentials."

means to fail in order to move on. That is missing in this sector.

For industrialists among our readers, it may be interesting to note that Dr. Wolff-Hertwig received degrees in English studies and musicology, according to *Wikipedia*, before she began climbing the management ladder.

Germany, once a proud builder of nuclear power plants, is now decommissioning its advanced power generating capacity.

Heading into the Post-Industrial Society!

These comments raise the burning question: What is going on here?

The fact that the leaders of the energy industry are the ones promoting the new business model is no coincidence. We will show below that there is a logical, but disastrous connection between these two very particular German inventions, Industrie 4.0 and the so-called "energy transition." The position paper of the "Plattform Digitale Energiewelt" of the German Energy Agency from June 2016 clearly indicates that the primary purpose of the exaggerated debate on digitalization is to maintain a doomed-to-fail energy transition.

Two aspects are emphasized in the paper:

1. Digitalization is an important "enabler" for the energy transition.
2. Digitalization opens up strategic business areas in the energy sector.

Hans J. Schellnhuber

Both the first and the second of these points—and even more so both—will drive our economy into a brick wall *in the short term*. We will show below why that is the case.

Digitalization as an 'Enabler' For the Energy Transition

The reason why the German government uses the awkward English expression "enabler" in all its papers simply has to do with the fact they don't want to use the German word *Retter* ("rescuer") because that would un-

mistakeably imply that something has already gone seriously wrong. The decision to opt out of nuclear energy, the subsidies fixed by law and the preferential feeding-in of so-called "green" electricity have not only led to a doubling of electricity prices, but have also driven conventional power plants into bankruptcy.

The *Frankfurter Allgemeine Zeitung* wrote on Oct. 21, 2017:

As shown by an overview of the Federal Network Agency (*Bundesnetzagentur*), energy suppliers have so far requested the shutdown of 90 power units with a total capacity of nearly 20,000 megawatts. Of that, just under 13,700 megawatts are slated to be taken off the network for good, and the operators hope the electricity price will rise for the rest. A number of these shutdown application requests, in particular for the plants south of the Main River, were temporarily blocked by the Network Agency, due to fears of unsecured supplies.

However, the government's plans for "de-carbonization" of the economy call for getting rid of all those plants, and creating a "decentralized energy supply instead."

To gain an understanding of where we are headed, it is useful to look at the plans and visions of "top advisers" such as Hans J. Schellnhuber, and Jeremy Rifkin, who serve to guide both Chancellor Merkel and the EU and which will simply result in the destruction of our industrial society in favor of a post-industrial "sharing economy."[3]

The buzzwords for the allegedly possible implementation of these plans are smart meter, smart grids,

---

3. Cf. "Die Science Fiction des Jeremy Rifkin oder: die schöne neue Welt der Öko-Kollektive," *Neue Solidarität* 35/2017.

smart Internet, smart everything. It should be emphasized at this point that we do not intend to call into question the technology as such, for which there are certainly many sensible areas of application. The criticism is directed against the attempt, in a circuitous way, to rescue with technical means something which can no longer be rescued.

That is clearly confirmed in the "Plattform Digitale Energiewelt" of June 2016: "Digitalization Will Fundamentally and Permanently Determine the Further Development of the Energy Sector." On page 11:

cc/The Blackbird (Jay Black)

Homeless man in Canada.

> Digitalization will provide the essential solutions for being able to successfully implement the second phase of the energy transition in the strained interplay of security of supply, efficiency and environmental sustainability. It is important to integrate greater amounts of renewable energies effectively at market and system levels. That requires networking a multitude of decentralized units in order to optimize production and consumption by region and by time, by making use of the flexibility available. Innovative grid operating equipment, decentralized management approaches but also more extensive optimization and coordination of grid management over various voltage levels profit from digital solutions and allow the high level of flexibility and efficiency in further use of the grid, that is required for the integration of greater shares of renewable energies.[4]

Windmills in Mississauga, Ontario, Canada.

windontario.ca

It is striking that all these government papers infer that the aim is increased efficiency and optimization. Precisely the opposite is true. When power plants that are efficient regardless of weather conditions are replaced by windmills and photovoltaic technologies that are not only dependent on the weather but operate on medieval energy density levels, these new systems will never be efficient or optimal. Even laymen should realize that this whole transition will skyrocket electricity prices to unimagined levels.

A leading Canadian thinktank, the Fraser Institute, issued a study in October 2017, which examines the "Green Economy" in the Canadian province of Ontario.[5] The study not only confirms this trend, but sounds the alarm bells. It should be noted that Ontario has served as a kind of testing ground for green energy policy outside of Germany. With the Ontario Green Energy and Green Economy Act of 2009, the decision was taken to implement the whole shebang, that is, even measures that are expected to be implemented only little by little in Germany. The study found that in addition to the drastic expansion of windmills, photovoltaic installations and biogas plants, so-called smart technologies for homes and production facilities were introduced (the "Green Button Program") and coal-powered plants were shut down. In a matter of a few years, the electricity price rose by 50%, resulting in an 18% decline in manufacturing output and a 28% drop in

---

4. Cf. https://shop.dena.de/fileadmin/denashop/media/Downloads_Dateien/esd/9163_Grundsatzpapier_der_Plattform_Digitale_Energiewelt.pdf

5. Fraser Institute, Vancouver, Study Oct. 2017: "Rising Electricity Costs and Declining Employment in Ontario's Manufacturing Sector."

employment.

The Fraser Institute study draws the alarming conclusion that 64% of the manufacturing jobs lost could be attributable to rising electricity prices, and that for every new job created under the "green energy" initiative, nearly two manufacturing jobs were lost. The study states: "Ontario's manufacturing sector accounts for almost 40% of Canada's exports, so its decline is a matter of national concern." One can only hope that the Fraser Institute study will be given the attention needed, and in time to prevent a similar decline in the productive medium-sized enterprises here in Germany.

New Strategic Lines of Business?

Does the goal and scope of the green expansion deserve to be called "smart?" Are these really new viable business models?

The crucial phrase in the Bitkom fact sheet is: "As reality already shows, the actual revolution of Industrie 4.0 does not occur in production, but in the business models."

We have already heard that business models such as those of UBER, Google, Netflix, Airbnb and a few other Internet giants could provide the basis for such success for former major energy producers. Their primary concern in the future will no longer be to generate electricity, but rather to manage the large volumes of data that are produced as a result of the dismantling of our energy systems. Under the heading "Big Data," the "Plattform Digitale Energiewelt" states:

Large volumes of data are generated at various points in the energy world; technical units and players are constantly communicating with each other and among themselves. Big data is the gen-

creative commons

Decentralized energy supply: Rooftop photovoltaic panels in Berlin.

eration and the targeted pooling and analysis of voluminous data through the use of digital techniques. The targeted analysis of these data volumes presents a significant potential for the further development of business models. That potential can then be considerably increased by linking it to other data and with real-time assessments.

One example is the merging of current data production with additionally purchased weather forecasts and historical market data, in order to optimize one's own generation portfolio, so that greater revenues can be generated in the power and heating markets. In the current era of digitalization, data is a valuable asset for companies. In light of the immensely voluminous data, the challenge is to be able to create "smart data" out of big data by means of (semi) automated means of evaluation.[6]

UWI Group

40 MW solar array in Brandis, Germany.

What does that mean, simply put? Households as well as companies will have to hire a management agency in the future for their energy consumption. In Ontario, this model, which was adopted back in 2013, has been given the trendy name "the Green Button Alliance" and applies not only to electricity, but also to gas and water. The customer gives the data on his consumption to a company, has his ecological footprint measured, and is then managed and also—no one could be so naïve as not to assume so—surveilled. In return, he enjoys the advantage of being informed of the times when the energy supply is particularly low-priced (when the wind is blowing, for example) and of being

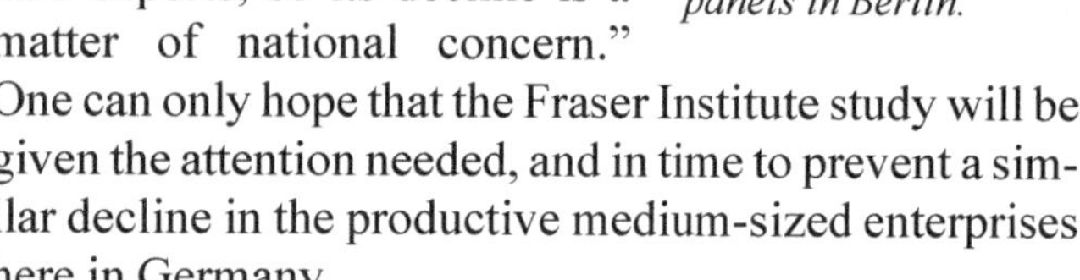

---

6. See footnote 2.

given special care in the event of blackouts.

EnergyLab 2030, a project of the CDU's Economic Council, proposes this model for Germany in a report titled, "A Renewable Energy System Needs Greater Adaptability from Producers and Consumers." The report states:

> With a view to expansion of the "Internet of Things" (IoT), European minimum standards on security, data interfaces and data protection should be defined to allow new business models, products and services and to reliably protect existing infrastructure against abuse.
>
> To allow energy data to be stored and released securely, in encrypted form and nearly in real time, a platform on the model of the "U.S. Green Button Initiative" should be established. That brings transparency and lays the basis for new services and products. The owner of the data alone must be able to decide who uses his data and how.[7]

The public is led to believe that these broker agencies represent a completely new value-added chain, and that a completely new online corporate world is being created that can generate huge profits without producing anything. When was the last time we heard that? Exactly 20 years ago, reputable "experts" such as Mortimer B. Zuckerman and others were proclaiming the birth of the post-industrial society in America, that America controlled the world of Internet platforms and that the "new economy" was the new paradise. It was repeated everywhere, parrot-like, and many people invested their savings in such start-ups, but by March 2000 the "new economy" was over. Do energy producers today really hope to pull that same old rabbit out of the hat again?

This type of business model, then as now, has noth-

creative commons

Post-industrial Germany: Kalkar, former experimental fast-breeder nuclear reactor site, now an amusement park.

ing to do with creating value. It is the same old mistake that has plagued our economic theories for over 50 years: Making a lot a money does not mean creating value. Don't we see that China is investing gigantic sums in the development of the physical economy and is much better off because of that? And that the success of the Belt and Road Initiative might have something to do with that, and that the building of railways, airports, maritime ports and industrial parks actually creates real value? Why are the top managers of our previously major utilities so stupid as to assume that post-industrial Internet businesses can be more promising than an operating power plant?

But to turn to such business models in the current situation is particularly catastrophic, because those models have been devised in the context of the dismantling of one of the cheapest, safest and environment-friendly energy systems. The upshot: What is praised as a solution is doubly wrong. Neither the technology installed to rescue the energy transition, nor the post-industrial business models are smart or sexy, they are downright unprofessional and will not last long for that reason.

The great benefits of digitalization, however, will be closely linked to the development of the real economy, which does not serve monetary special interests, but people.

---

7. EnergyLab 2030 des Wirtschaftsrats, presented at the 15th Klausurtagung "Energy and Environment" on March 10, 2017.

LaRouche's Four Laws for Italy's Recovery

Feb. 6—On March 4, Italy will vote again in parliamentary elections to form a new national government and new regional governments in Lombardy and Lazio. This is the first election after an electoral reform, the so-called "Rosatellum." Former Premier Renzi was only able to impose this reform after eight votes of confidence in the Chamber of Deputies and the Senate, since there was so much opposition to the reform among all the parties. Speaker of the Senate Pietro Grasso left Renzi's Democratic Party after these votes, and formed a new party, *Liberi e Uguali*, which is now running against the Democratic Party.

The reform requires a majority of 40% of the popular vote in order to form a government, and was designed to prevent Italy's biggest party, the Five Star Party (which will probably get around 28% of the vote) from being able to form a government—creating that situation of ungovernability, which, as Liliana Gorini, chairwoman of Movisol writes in the statement we publish below, "is the way the financial oligarchy keeps control over Europe."

The other parties have formed coalitions in order to reach the required 40%. A right- wing coalition includes Berlusconi's *Forza Italia*, Salvini's *Lega*, and Meloni's *Fratelli d'Italia*, and a so-called center-left coalition includes Renzi's Democratic Party, a list led by Emma Bonino significantly called "More Europe," and two other small lists (*Insieme*, and *Civica Popolare*, the latter led by the present Health Minister Lorenzin). Already, Premier candidates are announcing that if they do not reach the required 40%, new elections will be needed.

As Gorini explains in her statement, the main themes of the election campaign are: 1) obedience to the *diktat* of the European Union in order to be allowed to form a government (Berlusconi went to Brussels to assure them that his government will stick to the Maastricht parameters, while Emma Bonino went so far as to propose a spending freeze in order to pay the debt); and 2) a very strong anti-refugee campaign by almost all parties, with violent racist tones from Lega candidate Salvini, which led to the shooting of six African refugees in Macerata, where a former Lega candidate shot them in the street, and made the fascist salute after his criminal deed.

Apart from a public speech by Premier candidate Luigi Di Maio (Five Star Party) in Mestre about Glass-Steagall, there has been no discussion in this campaign about banking separation, the New Silk Road, or any other measure which would truly revive the Italian economy, and create new jobs. This despite the fact that the Italian banking system is almost bankrupt as a result of the European Central Bank (ECB) policy of encouraging financial speculation, and that in 2015 two pensioners committed suicide after losing their life savings as a result of the *salva banche* (save the banks) decree of Renzi's government.

Liliana Gorini, who chairs Movisol, LaRouche's movement in Italy, had been asked to run in this election with a citizens' list of candidates, on a platform similar to the one LaRouche PAC is now presenting for the mid-term elections in the United States. Thanks to Renzi's electoral reform and to the *Lega*, her citizens' list was sabotaged. She nevertheless wrote a candidate's statement asking all the other candidates to endorse her five points—four of them derived from LaRouche's Four New Laws, and the fifth the New Silk Road—as the only way to revive the Italian economy and solve the refugee crisis.

Five Principles to Revive Italy's Real Economy

by Liliana Gorini, chairwoman of Movisol, LaRouche's movement in Italy

This was supposed to be a candidate's statement. I was asked to run in the regional elections on March 4th with a citizens' list, in order to bring to the regional government council the experience of Movisol and of Lyndon LaRouche's movement internationally, to revive the real economy—starting with the reinstatement of the Glass-Steagall Act as it has long been proposed by LaRouche's movement in Italy, France, and the United States. Unfortunately, the citizens' list was sabotaged by one party.

The unhappy electoral reform imposed by Renzi (the so-called *Rosatellum*), aims at preventing new ideas, at maintaining the status quo, and at creating instability, since the financial oligarchy is enabled by the political instability of all European countries, and only keeps its speculative bubble alive thanks to the lack of courage of our governments.

Let's not forget that the speculative bubble is the cause of the economic crisis and of the growing poverty in Europe (with five million poor in our country alone). The policies of the EU and the ECB, including Quantitative Easing, aim at rescuing the big banks at the expense of depositors and tax-payers, as was demonstrated by the cases of the Veneto banks and of Monte dei Paschi di Siena. Deutsche Bank alone holds a derivatives exposure of 55 trillion euro, fifteen times the German GDP. Only with strict separation between ordinary banking and speculative banking, will it be possible to invest in the real economy. Let the speculators, not the citizens, pay the high price of the crisis they have created.

And yet in this election campaign, as in the earlier one on Renzi's constitutional referendum, we see the usual pilgrimage of Italian Premier candidates to London or Brussels in order to get the *placet* (the sanction) of the financial oligarchy and the EU hierarchs. Silvio Berlusconi went to Brussels to assure them that his government will stick to the Maastricht parameters and the *diktat* of the European Union. Renzi has always been an obedient servant, the Leporello of the EU, and exactly like Brussels, he is more interested in saving the banks than the population. Luigi Di Maio of the Five Star Party, who had publicly endorsed Glass-Steagall and claims to want to fight the big banks, flew to the City of London in order to reassure the "investors." Emma Bonino, who supports Renzi with a list called "More Europe," proposes to freeze spending in order to pay the debt. Once again, Moscovici and the other EU hierarchs are interfering heavily in the election campaign, deciding who is acceptable and who is not acceptable in a government. And in order to get more votes, candidates are appealing to the lowest instincts, including racism and xenophobia. As Helga Zepp-LaRouche wrote some years ago, "one more step, and we will have lost our humanity."

It is not spending which should be reduced, it is financial speculation. For many years, Lyndon LaRouche has been known all over the world as the only economist who had foreseen the crisis of 2008 and proposed concrete solutions, first of all Glass-Steagall and investments in infrastructure. The tragic accident of Pioltello, near Milan, where three women lost their lives in a train crash, shows that investment in infrastructure is urgent. It is also the key to a true economic recovery, in Italy and all over the world.

The principles of LaRouche's Four Laws should be at the center of the program of every candidate, together with the great projects of the New Silk Road, which can not only revive the real economy, but which are also the only way to solve the refugee crisis by investing in Africa, as presently only China is doing. Only a "Marshall Plan for Africa and the Middle East," like the one proposed by the Schiller Institute, can solve the problem of the of refugees landing on our coasts. It will certainly not be solved by concentration camps financed by the EU in Lybia.

Here are the 5 points of Movisol's program for the legislative elections in March:

1. Immediately reinstate Franklin Roosevelt's Glass Steagall banking separation act, before the imminent collapse of Wall Street's latest financial bubbles.
2. Return to a national banking system, as originally defined by Alexander Hamilton. Only state credits can allow growth.
3. State credit towards high-technology and high-productivity employment, including the rebuilding of our infrastructure, starting with the earthquake areas.
4. Launch a crash program to develop fusion power and for space exploration.
5. Join the Belt and Road initiative proposed by China, and the great projects of the Maritime Silk Road, which is the key for our ports in Genoa, Trieste, and Venice, and to develop the Mezzogiorno (Southern Italy).

China has launched the largest infrastructure development project in human history. Already ten times bigger than the Marshall plan, the Belt and Road Initiative (The New Silk Road) is bringing dozens of nations together in "win-win" economic collaboration around massive infrastructure projects. Much of Asia is already involved, and the program is already expanding into Europe, Africa, and South America.

For many formerly colonized and so-called developing nations, this is their first real opportunity for modern development. For stagnating industrialized nations, this is a critical opportunity for a new era of rebuilding, advancing, and producing.

LaRouche's Four Laws and the New Silk Road, together with a program to revive classical culture, from Dante to Giuseppe Verdi, are the key for a new Renaissance in our country.

Even if we are not running in this election, we ask you to propose our-five point program to your candidate, and demand it be adopted.

www.ingramcontent.com/pod-product-compliance
Lightning Source LLC
Chambersburg PA
CBHW081852250726
48659CB00008B/2705